Know Thyself,

Be Thyself

Know Thyself,

Be Thyself

James McQuitty

A James McQuitty Book
First Published April 2018
This Edition July 2022

This book replaces both *Know Yourself* and *Be Yourself* by the author with revised and updated content

Many other books in both paperback and kindle formats by <u>James McQuitty</u> are for sale worldwide through <u>Amazon</u>

<u>Other titles include:</u>

<u>Adventures in Time and Space</u>

<u>Christianity: The Sad and Shameful Truth</u>

<u>Escape From Hell</u>

<u>Golden Enlightenment – Twenty Year Anniversary Edition</u>

<u>How Psychics and Mediums Work, The Spirit & the Aura</u>

<u>Immortality</u>

<u>Spiritual Astro-Numerology: The Complete Guide</u>

<u>The Evolvement of the Soul</u>

<u>The Reason Why You Were Born</u>

<u>The Spirit World Realms</u>

<u>The Wisdom Oracle: An Aid to Accessing Your Inner or Higher-Self Wisdom</u>

<u>Find the Author at Facebook:</u>

<u>https://www.facebook.com/mcquittybooks</u>

<u>https://www.facebook.com/jamesmcquittysharing</u>

Table of Contents

Opening Note	7

Part One
Know Thyself

Foreword	11

Introductory Teachings

1. Life *is* Eternal	16
2. Spirit Communication	24
3. The Spirit World	26
4. Spirit World Reunions	28
5. God *is* Life	30
6. No Judgement awaits in Spirit Life	32
7. Religions Have Zero Authority	34
8. Free-will and Natural Spirit Laws	39

Intermediate Knowledge

9. How Psychics and Mediums Work and the Aura	41
10. Positive Thinking and Prayer	46

Advanced Information

11. The Soul, Reincarnation and Karma	48
12. Earth-bound and Lower Levels	53
13. Spirit Guides and Angels	55
14. The Past, Present and Future	59

Part Two

Be Thyself

Introduction to Part Two 67

Earth's Programmers

15. Family 74

16. Schools and Teachers 84

17. Friends and Work Colleagues 91

18. Employers 94

19. Comedians 97

20. Media Marketing 101

21. Doctors and Drugs 103

22. The Clergy 106

23. Spiritualists and New-Agers 110

24. The Government 114

25. 'Royalty' 118

26. Bigger Issues 122

Final Thoughts 133

Addresses 134

Websites and Links 135

Recommended Reading 137

About the Author 139

Opening Note

This two part book, with some revisions, incorporates two of my titles: *'Know Yourself'* and *'Be Yourself'*. Additionally, I have included a number of photographs and images in this new edition.

Some of my other books, such as *Golden Enlightenment-Twenty Year Anniversary Edition* and *The Reason Why You Were Born* endeavour to teach of our spirit or soul nature. Part one of this new book, *Know Thyself* does likewise.

Speaking personally, on occasions I have read and in some cases re-read a number of spirit teaching books. I often find that they are reaffirming of my own understanding. In some cases they present answers and explanations in a slightly different way to each other, or approached from a different but equally valid perspective or angle. This I find gives one a more rounded and comprehensive understanding of our spirit nature and all things associated.

When re-reading spirit teachings it is surprising how much I find that I had either forgotten or that had somehow passed me by on a first read. But perhaps this is just me? The earthly mind certainly isn't as marvellous as the spirit mind.

I have mentioned reading spirit teachings because I want to encourage everyone to read as many good quality spirit teaching books as they can, and I don't simply mean my own humble efforts. I have included some *'Recommended Reading'* at the end of this book.

Reading spirit teachings serves a double purpose, not only is this educational to the earthly consciousness, it also raises one's spirit energies. The more often we do this the more easily or smoothly it enables us to retune to our higher spirit consciousness and benefit from its guidance. Personally, when reading spirit related material I often get a certain *energy feeling* around the crown of my head. I sense the presence of perhaps a spirit guide, or simply other spirit people who are taking an interested in what I am reading (or when I am writing), and no doubt encouraging this.

This is one reason why I enjoy reading spirit teachings and I, in turn, through my intuitive faculties and my studies, sincerely hope and believe that this has enabled me to gather sufficient understanding to share accurate and reliable information, principally through my books.

Part two of this book shares some of my observations and thoughts of how we might better be true to our inner self. In this, I am sure readers will find much to consider. In places they may even find it amusing? And there is nothing wrong with this. I love humour and anything that is basically harmless and makes people laugh and raises their spirits is fine by me.

However, more seriously, in this second part readers may, perhaps, also find some inspiration to encourage them to make some positive changes in how they approach life and interact with family, friends and other people? Or at least give them some 'food for thought' in this direction.

Naturally, we are all *free spirits* at all times, so the final decisions we make on absolutely everything in life are our own choice.

Have fun.

Part One:

Know Thyself

10

Foreword

Know Thyself was inscribed in the forecourt of the *"Temple of Apollo"* at Delphi in Greece.

The Temple is perhaps best known for being home to the sanctuary "oracle", the priestess who would "prophesise" while in a trance state.

In a sense, not much has changed in the centuries that have elapsed since those ancient times that date back well over two thousand years.

People are still consulting the "spirits" and quite often endeavouring to get some glimpse of their future 'destiny' and guidance as to their life purpose.

***

When I say, "***Know Thyself***", I, and no doubt all the wise people of ancient times, recognised this to mean oneself as a ***"spirit being",*** an immortal soul, who can never die.

In the first part of this book, I will help those readers who are unfamiliar with spirit teachings by sharing my understanding. In fact, I will begin doing so immediately by saying that, basically, physical life is a *"temporary experience",* while our eternal *"Spirit individuality" is* the *"real self".*

We truly are *immortal souls*!! However, if this teaching or concept is an unfamiliar one to any reader, I would urge them not to dismiss this. Especially I would urge every reader not to confuse it as the propaganda of any religion. *It is a fact.* This is far more important to recognise, and especially its implications, than the limited understandings of any manmade religion.

"Thank God that life is eternal and that we are all immortal beings", we should all say! Because when we look around at how much some people on this planet suffer, if this physical life was all there is, many lives would undoubtedly seem, and sometimes be, very unfair!!

But of course there is much to discover about the spirit nature of *all* life. We can learn how in eternity things actually *do* balance out fairly, and that those who suffer now will also enjoy happy earthly lifetimes, and great joy in the spirit realms.

Spirit (or soul) information helps us to know ourselves as spirit beings. This is the focus of part one of this book. I feel it helps to have knowledge of our eternal nature, before reading part two. I say this because, 'armed' with this greater understanding, it can be hoped that readers will be encouraged and feel more empowered to give deeper consideration to how they live and express themselves in life. So that they may *truly be themselves*.

What I share In part two are some of my thoughts and feelings about a range of concerns. I sincerely hope that my thoughts, where necessary, will *'open the minds'* of *readers,* so that they too may delve into areas in life that, it seems, many people sadly never seem to give serious consideration to.

Perhaps what I have to say will help encourage some readers to better honour their true, inner self – which connects with their higher spirit consciousness, and to express this accordingly?

I believe that there is a need for us to 'wake up' and be true to ourselves. I say this because it seems to me that so many people live according to an agenda set by other people?

Through what I share readers may discover ways in which they may better live to suit their inner self desires? I hope so. This is more empowering and I am sure is what the soul would wish; it can also prove beneficial to the physical body.

The alternative is to follow or adhering to some party line or expected direction and mode of behaviour that may not be fully in harmony with the soul?

But who am I, the author?

Well, decades have passed since the early 1980's when I first began to seriously research the world of psychics and mediums, spirit and spiritual philosophy, complementary therapies, and all things associated.

During this time I have:

1. Received many evidential messages via mediums from relatives, friends and guides who reside in the spirit world realms.

2. Witnessed physical phenomena, and seen the faces of mediums transfigured by overshadowing spirit people.

3. Witnessed and experienced spirit surgery and healing with positive results forthcoming.

4. Received portraits of spirit guides who are my friends and mentors from the spirit realms – some with names independently verified by other mediums.

5. With my own eyes seen spirit people and animals on numerous occasions and heard the ringing of spirit bells – (and the latter phenomena was predicted before it ever happened).

6. Sat with mediums in a trance condition and conversed with spirit world guides who have communicated through them.

7. Studied the spirit philosophy and teachings given by many different spirit world communicators and recorded in numerous books.

Because of all that I have experienced and discovered I can confidently state that I accept the spirit information that I have included within *Part One* of this book as truth. In other words, at least as far as I am concerned, ***it is factual information.*** It contains no fiction, no make believe, no guesswork and no wishful thinking. Nor is it in any way, shape or form, reliant upon any system of faith, any religion, or religious beliefs or hopes. Although I must add that I am no "guru" or fountain of all knowledge, so it is always wise to seek one's personal "truth".

What I (and of course many others) do accept as factual, is some of the corroborated information received directly from highly reliable spirit world sources. In other words from people who, in times past, walked this Earth but who currently reside in higher dimensional states of spirit life that many would call "Heaven", or more appropriately, the "Spirit World".

It is therefore my strong opinion that readers can have total confidence in the validity of the information presented. However, I would and always do encourage everyone to seek further afield and to do their own investigative research. It is totally unnecessary to take my word alone, there are many sources of information 'out there'.

In part one I have included information about our spirit origins and much more. This contains some basic *Introductory Teachings,* followed by *Intermediate Knowledge* and then by more *Advanced Information.*

Naturally, there are some areas that overlap or merge with each other.

Part two of this book, as I said earlier, contains some of my personal thoughts and feelings about, *'how we might better express ourselves'.* Also, to encourage each of us to think more deeply about certain issues and to live and act honourably and in accord with our own higher-self, our soul.

It may be a surprise to some readers to learn that so many people do not truly live as freely as their soul might wish? However, I will say no more about this at this moment because part two contains its own introduction.

All that is left for me to say at this stage is "welcome" to a book that could, perhaps, prove highly enlightening to some readers? Particularly if there is a need and they consequently choose to 'take on board' what is said and act upon it in a positive way.

My wish, my deepest desire upon this planet, is for everyone to recognise that we are far greater than our physical bodies. Whether we use this knowledge to change our approach to certain 'earthly' situations so that we more wisely express ourselves is, obviously, our own decision to make.

Of course, some readers may already be living exactly how their inner self, their soul, wishes. If so, I offer them my sincere congratulations.

Finally, my advice to everyone is to "be happy" in the knowledge that, no matter what, "*we are all immortal souls*".

Introductory Teachings

1. Life *is* Eternal

As I have said in my other books and in one way or another already in this one, there is life after the death of the physical body.

We *are* all eternal-indestructible-immortal aspects of Source (or God) consciousness "Spirit beings", "Souls", with mind. We were so before the birth of our physical bodies, and we will continue to be so when our time to 'die' and depart Earth arrives. To the soul the physical body is like a heavy overcoat we wear for a limited time that weighs us down upon Earth. When we eventually remove it this fully releases us, the soul, to soar back to our spirit home world from whence we came.

We, the spirit beings that we are, have no reliance upon the physical body or its brain. The mind works through the brain while we are upon Earth. For analogy, the mind is like the entire Internet, containing far more knowledge and wisdom than can possibly flow through the brain which, by comparison, is the most basic of home computers and little more than a calculator. The spirit mind, when we can once again fully access it in the spirit world, is vastly superior.

In spiritual teachings the terms "spirit" and "soul" are often used to mean the same thing, and this is fine. It simply depends upon which term is preferred. The spirit is the power or energy that is present in all life, the human soul is the individualised spirit being.

New seekers may ask if there is proof of 'life after death?' The answer is yes.

It has been proven countless thousands of times throughout the centuries. Mediums worldwide prove it each and every day. People have always reported seeing, hearing, or feeling the presence of those who have 'passed on' or "died", as it is usually referred to.

Such reports are made constantly from all four corners of the globe. They come from people at all levels of society, from the financially wealthy and from the poor alike. They come from the devout followers of religion and from the atheist. They come from the intellectual academics as well as the average person on the street. Practically everyone knows at least one person who has had an experience of spirit contact. In the vast majority of cases reports are not based on imagination, illusions, or lies. They are factual experiences.

Many respected and open-minded scientists, doctors and university professors who have carried out research projects have also accepted the fact that life continues beyond the physical.

A great many different kinds of spirit communications have been scientifically examined. These include materialisations of spirit people, independent voice and spirit voices recorded on tape. They also include people who have had near-death experiences (NDE's), and met 'deceased' relatives and friends; and when sometimes the person who has the experience has seen and heard things that occurred well beyond the range of their unconscious or "dead" physical senses.

Some of these people have literally been pronounced "dead" by doctors because they had zero brain activity, and no heartbeat. There are even a number of cases when the spirit (or soul) of people pronounced dead has 'miraculously' returned to their physical bodies and they have regained consciousness to find themselves in a "morgue"!! Giving quite a fright to those in attendance. I remembering hearing one such chap saying how this happened to him after a very lengthy time away from his physical body, and it was as well that he returned when he did, because his body was scheduled for an autopsy!!

Spirit people have also communicated via radio, telephone, on television and computer screens and via answering and fax machines (I wonder if fax machines still exist anywhere?). Many people have spoken with or seen recognisable images of so-called 'deceased relatives' and friends in this way.

There are also many scientists working in the field of quantum physics who accept that survival of death is a natural part of physics. It has long been an accepted scientific fact that energy cannot be destroyed, it can only change form. The research now proves without a shadow of doubt that mind and consciousness are likewise aspects of indestructible energy.

A book I can recommend that details overwhelming scientific support is: *A Lawyer Presents the Evidence for the Afterlife* by Victor and Wendy Zammit.

Sadly, there are still some closed-minded sceptics who refuse to accept any evidence of continuous life. No matter if a loved-one materialised before them and told them things known only to the two of them, they would still refuse to accept the truth. (They would probably go to their doctor and say they had been hallucinating!).

I can only guess that such people, who quite commonly refuse all opportunities to personally investigate the overwhelming evidence with a fair and open mind, feel somehow threatened by the truth. But this will not stop it being the truth.

The Meaning and Purpose of Life, a book by my friend *Brian Sadler*, contains a list of dozens of great scientific and intellectual persons who during the last 150 years have researched life after death, mediums, materialisations, or other aspects of spirit communication or phenomena.

To name just a few from those listed in Brian's excellent book who have since passed to spirit, they include: John Logie Baird (TV pioneer), Sir William Crooks (a top Physicist), Sir Arthur Conan Doyle (Doctor and author), Air Chief Marshall Lord Dowding, Sir Oliver Lodge (a top Physicist, he also communicated after passing in books like, The Truth The Whole Truth and Nothing but the Truth, through the medium Raymond Smith), and Professor Charles Richet (a Nobel Prize winner). Numerous scientists and other eminent individuals who are still researching are also mentioned in the Brian Sadler and the Victor and Wendy Zammit books.

If any reader seeks personal proof the simplest route to take in the UK is to the nearest Spiritualist centre or church. Most of them hold demonstrations of 'mediumship' (often called clairvoyance); and even their Sunday services generally incorporate such a demonstration. The primary objective behind each demonstration is to prove the continuation of life through evidential messages from those so-called dead.

If one attends often enough it is highly likely that a 'spirit message' will be replayed to them, more often than not from a relative or friend who has 'gone home' to spirit life.

(Some mediums also take bookings for private consultations).

If one finds a medium elsewhere, via the Internet or advertising privately, for instance, please do be warned that just like in every walk or trade in life there are some outright con-artists. So there are some unscrupulous people who unfortunately give genuine mediums a bad name. There are also some sincere individuals of lesser mediumistic ability because, and once again, like in every trade, standards and abilities do vary.

Finally, some readers may wonder why 'life after death', as it tends to be called, is not openly accepted and acknowledge by the media and every scientist.

One reason is because most of the people who run so much of society are entrenched in highly materialistic or physical life concentrated lifestyles and beliefs, and this keeps their consciousness shut off from their spirit nature. They simply do not want to know and more or less 'bury their heads in the sand' as far as the spirit and spiritual nature of life is concerned. They are effectively addicted to the physical and material side of life and, like many a drug addict, fixated on this to the exclusion of consideration of anything else.

A worldwide media and scientific acceptance of life after death would be a dramatic and life changing experience that would impact upon the lives of every single person upon this planet. So many people would find this too frightening to contemplate. So they prefer to deny any possibility of anything but the physical realm.

If something comes along that challenges them to awaken and acknowledge the spirit side of life they shout their denial loudly. Many people do not want to acknowledge the truth because this represents a challenge to everything in their life - a scary prospect to face.

Speaking generally, those who are materially and financially at the top, wish to stay there. If they believe they need to treat those below them badly to maintain their power and lifestyle, they do so.

"All is fair in business", they say. But is it?

If by unscrupulous means a bigger business undermines a smaller one, causing it to fold, and all who work for that smaller business to lose their livelihood, is all really fair in business?

I think the individuals who suffer as a consequence of the bigger businesses actions find this very unfair.

It is highly likely that most people 'at the top' in business mistakenly believe that the physical life is all there is? Consequentially, they mistakenly believe that their actions bring no consequences other than to their physical lives.

If 'overnight' life after death was somehow acknowledged worldwide, to people such as the 'big business materialists' it would seem like an attack upon their integrity and agitate their conscience.

Especially when they learned that in the fullness of time, in the spirit life, they would have to face admitting their greed. Such a thought they dare not contemplate. Many therefore convince themselves that death is the end and refuse to contemplate any possibility that they may be wrong in this belief.

There are others amongst the materialists who have a vague believe in a 'heaven', but assume that they will face no consequences when they go there.

They may even convince themselves that by attending an orthodox church, such as a Catholic church, and asking for forgiveness of their sins and giving a contribution to the wealth of the church, they are cleared of all misdeeds and guaranteed a good afterlife reward?

Such people do like to fool themselves with such imaginings, because this is the only way they can cope and subdue their inner conscience.

So no matter what, it seems to me, that some people will never accept the truth that life has no endings – only new beginnings.

In fact, and of great regret to me, it seems that the vast majority of people do refuse all opportunities to learn or listen, or investigate or even contemplate the possibility of spirit communication, life after death, and the immortality of the soul. If only more people would 'wake up' to the spirit truth because it can and does enrich and generally make happier the lives of those who are spiritually awake.

Quite often the closed-minded sceptics who prefer to remain in the dark (and in a spiritual sense this can be quite literal darkness), even suggest that those who do accept that life is immortal and that life continues after the death of the physical body are deluded and gullible people.

But this is like a blind person telling us that no one can possibly see, and that vision is impossible, and that only the deluded and gullible would believe such a concept.

Sometimes such people are quite vocal and outspoken in their condemnation of the spirit nature of life. They try to convince others that there is no such thing. Yet, of course, their 'certainty' carries no authority because by their own admission they will never, with a truly open mind, investigate the overwhelming evidence because they think it is all a lie and that they will be wasting their time.

There is an old proverb that is quite apt, '*If the blind lead the blind, both shall fall into the ditch*'. Unfortunately, so many seem to prefer their self-made ditch.

I do not judge anyone. We may all have been ignorant to the spiritual facts of life in this or a past lifetime. So one day, in this lifetime or another, those in dark ditches will climb out into the light. I am simply endeavouring to share spirit truths in the hope that it will help those willing to open their minds to greater wisdom.

One reason I do so is because when such facts are accepted they help us to live more enlightened lives. This does make a great difference to us, firstly when we depart the Earth life, and also in our further progress in the spirit realms.

It is never too late to learn, and sooner is always better than later.

2. Spirit Communication

To receive a communication from someone physically deceased is quite natural.

It can only happen when a spirit person desires to communicate, although it isn't automatically easy for them to do so.

It helps greatly if the person or people on Earth are open-minded enough to see a medium, privately or at a public demonstration.

To receive a direct, and more physically obvious, communication from someone in spirit life, such as suddenly hearing a spirit voice or seeing a physically materialised person, may not always prove possible or even be desirable. I think that many people would be frightened to see a deceased loved one suddenly appear before them; although some people have experienced this.

However, because it can prove scary to those upon Earth, many spirit people would not attempt to put in an appearance, even if they possess the ability to do so.

There are many ways those in spirit life can communicate. The most common is to have their message relayed via a medium. Some of these mediums hear (called clairaudience), some see (called clairvoyance) and some feel (called clairsentience). Many receive a mix of all three.

There are also some mediums capable of going into a trance state to allow a spirit person to speak through them. Many wonderful books have been written of spirit teachings received in this way.

While there are also some exceptional mediums who can facilitate the materialisation of people visiting from the spirit world. In some cases in the circles of a "Physical medium", as such mediums are known, it has also been reported that animals have materialised. This proves that the continuation of life is natural for all life forms, and not solely for humans.

Materialised spirit people can sometimes seem as physically tangible as we feel to each other in the physical, and be equally solid to the touch.

Whereas, when a spirit person is seen shortly after their passing, by a relative or friend for instance, they may appear less solid and somewhat translucent, and naturally be capable of passing through material objects.

3. The Spirit World

All those people on Earth who live reasonably decent, respectful, kind, sharing, and loving lives, will find they gravitate to beautiful surroundings when they 'die' and return to the spirit world.

Over the years, many spirit communicators who reside there, have informed us about the environment in which they now dwell.

They tell us of its beauty, of flowers and trees, of their delightful homes, of an environment that is like a continuous yet gentle summer. Basically, they say that their world is like a utopian version of the Earth. They also speak of the peace, love and harmony they experience and much more.

It is a world in which the inhabitants can pursue their hearts desires, whether recreational, study, or service to others in numerous ways, or, of course, a mixture of each.

We are informed that the spirit world has many levels of life, from the high spiritual planes down to the lower undesirable levels, and that each is as real and tangible to the inhabitants as Earth feels to us.

There are many levels because each represents a different level of progression and consciousness. As inhabitants learn and progress they evolve to the next higher level of expression. Each is reportedly more refined, more vibrant, more beautiful and exhilarating to experience.

Whereas, for those who have 'gone too far astray' on Earth and, for instance, lived abusive, greedy, cruel or evil lives, they will find they gravitate to one of the lower levels of spirit life. My book, **Escape from Hell**, includes descriptions of just how bad some of these hellish levels truly are.

Readers who would like more details about the spirit world might also enjoy reading some good books by Anthony Borgia, such as *Life in the World Unseen*.

There are also many *Silver Birch* books that contain valuable information, such as *Silver Birch Companion*.

The spirit guide White Feather, is another wonderful source of communicated spirit teachings, and these come through the excellent trance mediumship of Robert Goodwin. *In the Presence of White Feather* is one of many books that contain his teachings.

Lastly, a book by the medium *Frederick C. Sculthorp* that contains plenty of interesting material obtained during "Astral Projection" (out of body experiences), is: *Excursions to the Spirit World*.

All of these and more are listed in *Recommended Reading* at the end of this book.

4. Spirit World Reunions

When we pass from the physical life, no matter our age, most of us, and I am speaking of people who have lived reasonably decent lives, Mr and Mrs Average we might say, are immediately greeted by one or more of those we love, whether relatives or friends. While for some it may be a spirit guide who we will soon recognise.

What will determine the level of the spirit world to which we naturally aspire, or are guided to, will be a reflection of the Earth life we have lived, and the level of consciousness we have attained.

Initially, however, if a need exists, some people are guided to an intermediary level of spirit life that allows them to adjust to their new environment and where they will receive emotional and mental healing. This can be necessary because for some their Earth life may have proven very draining on them, while for some the nature of their transition to spirit life can be dramatic and traumatising.

However, when all is well and once settled-in to life in the spirit world we are free to associate with whomsoever we wish, provided the desire is reciprocated. There, love in its purest sense, is in harmonious accord with the natural laws of attraction.

Therefore, we will have the opportunity to reunite or meet again with people we knew upon Earth and to make new friends. We may even meet people we had forgotten because, if they have fond memories of us, they may wish to say hello and welcome us.

We may also find 'old friends' from previous times in spirit life with whom we may have shared great friendships in past earthly lifetimes. (In due course of time, and this can vary, we will remember them and the previous lifetimes!).

If some of those we care for have progressed further, to higher levels than ourselves, they are still able to visit us.

Reunions can also occur with our beloved animal friends. Former pets, or companion animals, as they might better be called, since they also continue to live.

Naturally, this also applies to everything in nature; because everything is empowered by indestructible eternal spirit energy.

It is only the level of consciousness that varies. But all can and will gradually develop higher and greater degrees of consciousness. As indeed shall we.

5. God *is* Life

As most of us probably realise, around the world in different religions a number of different names are used to represent the power that is most often called "God". (The name "God" is derived from the word "Good").

Native Americans use the "Great Spirit" or the "Great White Spirit". Amongst other titles the "Source" and the "Creator", as well as the "Power", can also and rightly be used.

To keep things simple, as it is more familiar to most people, I have used the term "God" in this book, but it really does not matter which term is used.

God *is* life; the spirit energy, power and source. In fact, as readers may already gather, everything that exists, not only on Earth but throughout the universe and beyond, is a manifestation of this spirit energy. This, as I have said, includes people, animals, all in nature, and every planet and sun in the cosmos. 'Reality' as we experience it is created by universal sub-division of 'The One' energy (God), mind and consciousness.

Furthermore, spirit world teachers tell us that God *is* love; and that God acts through natural spirit laws.

There is no personified God. If we wish to see God we can look at nature and at the stars in the cosmos on a clear night, and look within, look everywhere there is beauty, or whatever we perceive as beautiful, and we effectively see a glimpse of God.

Our soul, mind and spirit energy are therefore also aspects of God. So we can rightly be considered as Gods in miniature; or as children of God.

Yet nobody, whether on Earth or in the spirit world, can fully know God. Although the higher we progress the closer we become and the more we might feel the presence, our unity with God, and we may feel the power, and ourselves express greater and greater degrees of love.

6. No Judgement awaits in Spirit Life

When we physically die and arrive in the spirit world we will find no judge or jury waiting for us. There is no such thing as eternal punishment or damnation. The spirit world is full of compassion.

However, we will effectively judge ourselves because the realm to which we will aspire will be according to natural law, by our personal energy vibrations. All energy, including the soul, has a vibration, this is a frequency that represents, or corresponds, with progression. The faster the vibration the higher the soul has evolved.

Consequently, our soul vibration upon passing will indicate our level of attainment and reflect the lifetime we have lived. Those who by their own thoughts and actions have lived a more enlightened or loving lifetime have higher vibrations, so naturally they will gravitate to higher realms. While those amongst us who have committed acts we might deem abusive, cruel, wicked or evil, with correspondingly lower vibrations, will be drawn to darker and far less desirable realms.

Be assured that there is no damnation to an eternal hell ruled by any devil, and certainly not in the sense portrayed through certain religions. However, there are lower and darker realms, as I alluded to earlier, and these are sometimes called the shadowlands or simply low and darker levels. Although some spirit people do indeed refer to these dark realms as "Hell". (Readers of *Escape from Hell* may well find the term highly justifiable!).

So it is as a consequence of their thoughts and actions upon Earth, that some people do indeed find themselves at such levels when they pass from the physical life.

However, these souls are never forgotten or abandoned, there are those in spirit life who attempt to reach them and encourage them to begin their climb out of the miserable surroundings of these lower levels.

The climb begins when such a soul shows remorse and a desire to learn, serve and make recompense for what they have done. It is not judgement or punishment but a process of learning to awaken and express the goodness and love that lies within each and every soul, no matter how deeply buried.

If one thinks about it, there have been examples of inner potential in many a murderer or rogue (to say the least). Some have inflicted all sorts of suffering on strangers yet they have remained kind and loving to their mother or to their pet animal, for instance. Even the smallest flame of love can gradually be encouraged, giving even those in the lowliest of spirit levels the impetuous to make the effort to change and climb the spiritual ladder of progress.

7. Religions Have Zero Authority

In the same way that religions have misled people by wrongly claiming that there is a judgement day, they have fed society many miscomprehensions and even told deliberate outright lies.

Here are some facts to ponder...

- **Fact:** No religion holds any spiritual or heavenly power or authority.

- **Fact:** No religion can offer (or sell) forgiveness, or bestow any special rites of passage upon anyone.

- **Fact:** No religion has the authority to condemn anyone.

- **Fact:** No religion can take away or deny our spiritual birthright.

- **Fact:** Religions divide rather than unite people.

- **Fact:** Historically, religions have caused more wars than any other force that has or ever will exist on this Earth.

Even today some 'religious' fanatics continue to fight what they call 'holy' wars; and remain just as 'happy' as their ancestors to inflict acts of zealous butchery and barbarism.

The Christian religion tortured, burned or drowned mediums, natural healers and anyone else they feared or took a dislike to calling them witches or heretics (non-believers).

They deliberately set out and continue to make people fearful of communications with those who have passed-on, saying that mediums call up evil spirits or the devil (a fictitious figure).

At the same time, they have offered safe havens to paedophiles and even sadistic nuns. While in some countries nuns have even been raped by predatory priests. (See my book: *Christianity: The Sad and Shameful Truth*) They have done so very much purely for their own benefit; while working in conjunction with monarchs and dictators the world over as and when it suited them to do so.

The facts so far given should be enough to convince any sane person that to follow *any* religion is madness. The origins of religion can be traced back to nature worship, and my book (mentioned above) says more on this.

The following facts may also highlight the madness of accepting or following the Christian religion...

- **Fact:** Jesus never started the religion of Christianity. It developed after his time upon Earth!

- **Fact:** Before the Roman Catholic Church (formerly the Roman Empire!) elevated Jesus to 'son of god' status at the council of Nicaea in 325 AD (approximately 300 years after his physical death), declaring Christianity as the new state religion, there were at least 16 other religions that, in their teachings, elevated one character to this same status of 'saviour'.

- **Fact:** Mithraism was the state religion of Rome before Christianity took its place. Until this time Mithra (not Jesus) was considered to be the 'son of god', 'born of a virgin', and basically the exact same story as they teach about Jesus.

It can therefore be concluded that there is nothing new or unique about Christianity and that in reality it is a copycat of older religions.

Here is a final fact...

- **Fact:** No one knows for sure which culture first told the fable of the 'saviour' or 'son of god', although the oldest recorded in modern history is Osiris, something like 4000 years ago in Egypt. The old myths of the past were then rewritten and draped around the newly selected 'saviour'. This fable was applied to Jesus (who most assuredly was a spiritual teacher, medium and healer who, it seems certain, was in attunement with his own higher-self consciousness. A truly good and enlightened chap! – As I'm sure he still is!).

When a religion sets itself above the people, in a position of dogmatic control, telling people what to think and how to behave, it transgresses from a potentially helpful source of guidance to a hindrance upon society.

When religions insist on their own blind dogma (belief) and instil fear in their followers to suppress them from seeking their own truth, this, more or less, *is* indoctrinated mind control.

Religions such as Christianity attempt to keep us in fear of personal investigation because they realise that if people do seek for themselves they will very soon discover the truth, that life is eternal, regardless of which if any religion is followed. They also realise that this will threaten their power, control and wealth, including future income, because it is a massive global branded business.

Some good books to read to understand more about the origins of religion include: *The Faiths, Facts and Frauds of Religious History* by Emma Hardinge Britten; *The Rock of Truth* by Arthur Findlay; and *When Prophets Spoke* by Rev. Maurice Elliot.

It may also interest readers to see what was said in a spirit communication from *"Menno"* in a lovely little book titled, *A Guide Book to The Land of Peace,* by Mary Countess Van Limburg Stirum. He said this in a message on the night of February 7th, 1955.

'There is a tendency in your world today, to take life lightly, and to put aside serious thoughts, especially religious ones. Of those who go to church, many go feeling that they have been very good and have fulfilled all their religious duties by going, and then forget about it for the rest of the week. Also many people have a dislike of talking about such things, fearing to have their very comfortable religious ideals disturbed, or because they might find some reason

for looking more closely at their own thoughts and actions.

*'How much better it would be for many people, if they would **look more deeply into themselves**, and face clearly their attitude to religion.*

'What is religion? Loving God, which means loving all that is good and beautiful and helpful to others, but most people don't want to risk the thought "I might have helped that one and I did not do it." They prefer to put off the thought lightly, in order to avoid realising that it is true.

*'Face up to life - **study yourself** - know where your faults lie and study them. Don't shrug your shoulders, and think of something which seems more pleasant to you.*

*'In the old religions, there was a saying **'Know thyself'**. If you can do this, then you have reached the point of being able to progress and climb a little higher along the path.'*

I hope that this book is helping readers to know themselves as far more than a physical being. While part two of this book may help readers to better **be themselves.**

8. Free-will and Natural Spirit Laws

We each have free-will so how we choose to live our life on Earth is our own affair.

However, as I have already as good as mentioned, what we do *is* of great importance because repercussions, **for better or worse,** will be forthcoming.

In the spirit life, just as on Earth, we will not be told what to do.

There are though natural limitations, determined by our degree of progression, which is reflected in our level of consciousness.

For instance, in spirit life we cannot simply choose to visit or enter a higher level of expression – we have to reach an appropriate level of consciousness to do so.

Alternatively, we may be guided for a temporary visit to a higher level for a particular reason, and this would be by someone from that or a still higher level of expression. This, quite likely, would be to teach us something or to encourage us to strive for our own greater progression.

Spirit teachers often speak of the natural laws that operate and affect everyone. One major law is "cause and effect". Basically it is like a boomerang effect. What we give out, that is do, say or even think, will always return to us in some way, shape or form.

As an example, those who abuse others, steal, suppress and unjustly control and so forth, will in time need to face the 'negative energies' that such behaviour creates. These may only become apparent to them when they pass-on, but in time (and we have eternity) they will find that they have 'reaped according to how they have sown'. In other words, what goes around comes around. This is natural law and it cannot be avoided.

Naturally, this applies equally to actions, words and thoughts of a kind, loving, generous and uplifting nature. What we would consider 'good'. Such a lifetime will reap accordingly.

The law, as I am endeavouring to make crystal clear, is not a judgement, but the outworking of natural law. If we choose to ignore the inner direction of conscience, which seeks to guide us in a loving way, then natural law will effectively teach us.

It is our choice; God never interferes or judges in any way, it is always left for us to learn by our own volition.

Intermediate Knowledge

9. How Psychics and Mediums Work and the Aura

Much of what I say in this section is also covered in my book: *How Psychics and Mediums Work, the Spirit and the Aura,* although that book may contain more detailed information.

I find it necessary to include again for those who solely read this book, so that they can gain sufficient understanding of 'how these things work'. I hope those who have read the earlier book can appreciate this.

***

Psychics have a heightened awareness which enables them to sense thoughts or feelings through vibrations. All of us are psychic to degree and have, for instance, sensed when someone is approaching us from behind. Or sensed when someone is staring at us, even if across a room or from the other side of some street. What allows us to sense someone in these examples is our own aura which is our personal energy field.

Basically, when someone approaches us from behind his or her energy touches our energy, and we sense that they are there. Across a room, or even across a street, someone staring will project energy, most generally without realising that they are doing so and, if projected sufficiently, again this will touch our own energy field and alert us. We all project and receive energy signals, usually without recognition of doing so.

More professional psychics may use "psychometry", which generally involves handling objects, such as a ring, necklace, bracelet or wristwatch worn regularly by the person they are attempting to glean information about.

They do so by attuning to the vibrations which are effectively stored in the molecules and atoms of the items, and in their etheric (or spirit) counterparts, and everything material has such a counterpart. Strong emotions in particular can generate vibrations which can become embedded in the very fabric of items, or indeed in the walls of buildings and the surrounding atmosphere. This is why a psychic can enter an historic building where something tragic or violent occurred and sense this.

However, a psychic who has not developed any mediumistic abilities cannot consciously contact those who have passed-on.

***

Mediums, who work using clairvoyance, clairaudience or clairsentience, or a combination of these, are firstly able to do so because they have the ability to raise their own vibrations to a higher frequency. This enables those from the spirit side of life, who lower their vibrations to a similar rate as achieved by the medium, to link telepathically and mentally project images, thoughts and feelings to the medium.

This can happen and seem quite natural to some mediums, and may require very little if any conscious effort on their part. Whereas, many mediums achieve this higher vibrational link after they have said a prayer, and/or a desire to be of service - a thought with higher aspirations.

Such a link sounds fairly straightforward and easy to establish but, of course, it is not. Vibrations change according to how and what we think. Therefore they can change and fluctuate very quickly and weaken the telepathic mental link.

Spirit communicators seeking to pass a message via a medium also vary in experience; and likewise their attunement may wander from the desired frequency – particularly if excited about a first communication with a loved-one on Earth.

When messages are successfully relayed they still require the medium to be able to interpret them correctly. Some hear thoughts like a voice, but many others receive an impression of a thought, and they need to recognise the difference between a communicator's thoughts and their own.

With images they have to intuitively recognise any symbolic meaning, and know which are literal. The reason why symbolic imagery is used is because it is far easier to telepathically transmit and receive a single image, like a single photograph, than the equivalent of a video film. (Just as photos on a computer take less space and are easier to send than videos). Therefore, this is particularly suitable if one image can relay sufficient meaning.

Feelings too can be tricky, to recognise that a sudden feeling is, for instance, how someone communicating felt just before they passed-on, and not something actually happening within their own body.

Combining all that they receive and delivering it as a coherent message to recipients takes experience. For instance, it may take some time for a medium to mentally build their own recognition of what a single image appearing in their minds-eye symbolically means. They often do this gradually in cooperation with their spirit guides.

On occasions mediums do encounter difficulties and even the better exponents are, like all of us, prone to "off days". Mediums are literally attempting to communicate with people who are living in a different dimension of eternal life. In many ways it is incredible and to their credit that so many of them are able to receive and interpret as well as they do.

Some mediums are more naturally sensitive than others; so standards of mediumship do vary quite considerably, as I detailed in my book that I mentioned earlier.

Although, the 'bottom line' is that communication through mediumship *can* (and regularly *does*) provide a genuine link with those who have passed-on to the spirit world.

What is commonly called the "Aura" is actually an enveloping of spirit "energy fields" (alternatively called "energy bodies") which interpenetrate each other and link with the physical body. Basically, they are part of our spirit energies which motivate (or empower) our physical bodies.

These energies flow to glands and organs and throughout our physical body via what acupuncturists and other complementary therapists call the "chakras" (also known as "energy centres") and along what are referred to as "meridian pathways". For analogy these meridians can be likened to arteries and veins, but instead of carrying blood they carry energy.

When we pass-on our auric energies return to spirit life with us and constitute part of our spirit body.

Several energy fields are named in various books, although the names do vary depending upon the teacher. These include the Etheric, Astral, Mental, and Spiritual fields. But in my opinion it is best not to be too dogmatic about names because, as I have said, these do vary and are only names.

In the spirit life the lower fields of the aura that we initially take with us dissolve when no longer necessary, and particularly when we move up to higher levels of the spirit world. They become superfluous to our needs. However, meaningful memories are always retained.

For more information on the aura, chakras and energy then, amongst others, *The Golden Thread* (chapter two) from a selection of informative books by Robert Goodwin with the teachings of White Feather can be read.

10. Positive Thinking and Prayer

The power of thought is used to create everything in the spirit life. We are spirit beings here and now, even though we are presently functioning through a physical body.

On Earth most if not all of us lack the more accomplished development and creative control of our thoughts and spirit energies that can be achieved in the spirit life. Nonetheless, our thoughts *do* project energy that also registers in our own aura or energy field.

When one remembers what I said earlier about natural laws and cause and effect, then we may more readily grasp the concept of how and why good and constructive positive thinking and prayer can work for us, and why negative thoughts can prove detrimental to our progression, and even harmful to our physical bodies.

Positive thoughts of a suitable nature will potentially draw positive constructive outcomes; although upon Earth results can seem rather slow to manifest. One reason for this is because the physical dimension in which we currently live is a far slower and denser level of vibration than the spirit realms. However, to be totally effective positive thoughts need to be in accord with our state of progression and life purpose.

There are some people who mistakenly believe that if they can hold a 'positive' thought or image tenaciously, that this will draw their desired outcome to them. Usually, this is a desire to win the lottery, or for a new car, more money or some other want. Such thoughts are generally far from altruistic, and in effect they can be quite negative, as all that carry even a tinge of greed invariably must be. In other words dogmatic thoughts do not equal positive thoughts, often quite the reverse. The error people are perhaps making is to confuse powerful concentrated thoughts with positive ones. Yet if one thinks about it, many a tyrannical leader of nations or groups of one sort or another has proved far removed from being a good and decent person.

Prayer is a transmission of our thoughts; if it is virtuous, for instance a healing prayer for someone, then this will draw assistance from spirit healers or helpers. It will do so because strong thought transmissions are heard or recognised and noble requests attract many good souls who are happy and willing to be of service.

Therefore, if used wisely and positively thoughts and prayers can be utilised for the good of all.

Advanced Information:

11. The Soul, Reincarnation and Karma

Upon Earth no one (other than perhaps a genuine spirit master) can truly know their soul totality self, one's complete individualised soul, completely. This is because we, the higher-self or true soul, are far greater spirit beings than the earthly personality self can fully grasp and recognise.

The natural home of the "higher-self" or "higher-soul" or "soul totality" (all the terms mean the same thing) is in the spirit realms. Whereas the people we are on Earth are "facets" or "aspects" of our soul totality empowered by a percentage of our higher-soul energies.

As may be gathered, the higher-soul is effectively divisible, enabling some of its energy, mind and consciousness to function through a physical form, while the rest remains in the spirit realms.

As already mentioned, the "nucleus" of the soul that resides in the spirit world is often referred to as the "Higher-self". So rather than bombarding readers with a selection of terms that mean the same thing, from herein I will endeavour to use the term "higher-self" to represent the soul in spirit.

Each person's higher-self has provided the soul energy which currently motivates our physical bodies. When we pass from the Earth life, in the fullness of time, our consciousness will expand beyond the needs and desires of the spirit form of the personality. At this point our energies will once again flow consciously in conjunction with our own higher-self. (This is nothing to worry about, it is natural, and in many respects it is little different from waking from sleep to remember who we truly are).

At all times the physical person on Earth remains energetically linked to their higher-self, which is why previous lives, or incarnations, undertaken by aspects of the higher-self can sometimes be recalled or accessed under hypnosis, in dreams, or whilst in meditation. It also explains why young children are sometimes born with past life memories.

The higher-self resides at the level of vibration that has been reached by progression in the spirit realms and by the experiences that it has gained through incarnations by aspects of itself in physical form.

So our higher-self may have gathered wisdom from many different time periods in the history of this planet. Furthermore, experience of different forms and genders is nothing new to the higher-self. Each lifetime is viewed in much the same way as an actor views different roles they play.

What is generally termed "Reincarnation", as may be gathered, is really the undertaking of different physical embodiments by aspects of the higher-self energies.

Symbolically, the process of one aspect returning to the higher-self has been described as like returning a draft of liquid to a bottle and shaking it, so the next draft or aspect to emerge is never the exact same as any previous.

Rebirth, as it can also be called, is by some referred to as the karmic wheel of life from which there is no escape until we have gained a sufficient degree of enlightenment.

When incarnate we generally carry no conscious memory of past incarnations. Quite often such memories would be a burden and, if we did consciously remember them, they might only confuse us. Let's face it, if the earthly personality were fully to consciously recollect a lifetime as a man if now a woman, or vice-versa, or any negative actions undertaken in other lifetimes, this would rarely benefit them in their current physical lifetime.

Past physical lifetimes (or "incarnations") are like pieces of a jigsaw that at the appropriate time join together to give the higher-self a composite picture of progress.

We are informed by spirit guides that the higher-self, in spirit life, can project any personality it wishes. This may particularly occur if it was a 'favourite' lifetime or to pass messages to those the particular personality knew upon Earth. The personality aspect of any higher-self can effectively 'step forth' from the higher-self because it is never lost or erased. It is just that us spirit beings are far more, and far grander and greater, than any single earthly personality.

As I have already mentioned, there are natural spirit laws that operate; one is known as the "Law of Karma". Basically, if we harm no one deliberately, try to express love, are considerate, compassionate, and kind and forgiving to ourselves as well as to others, and follow the inner guidance of our intuition and conscience, then we will be living in harmony with the spirit laws.

Obviously, the above is a 'tall order' to constantly master and to live by. So no one should be too hard on themselves for their shortcomings, we can only do our best.

However, if we live opposite to the law our vibrations are lowered and this hinders our progress and creates negative karma that in time will need to be redressed or rebalanced.

The term karma is sometimes misinterpreted as fate or punishment, but it is neither. There is *no* pre-determined fate (other than the fact that one day the physical body will die, as we call it), because we all have free-will and, as I said earlier, there is no punishment.

At our higher-self level of consciousness we do not think with the limited conceptions of the earthly mind. If in one lifetime a karmic imbalance was caused then the higher-self may choose to redress or rebalance the situation and its energies through a future incarnation.

Someone without spiritual understanding may regard the concept of accepting an incarnation where one is physically challenged (blind, deaf, or unable to walk, for instance), as madness. But from the higher-self point of view the choice can make complete sense.

At the higher-self level of awareness we understand the benefits of each and every challenge we choose to accept. We are able to effectively view each lifetime as another acting role, each of which in due course will to the eternal soul seem no more than a mere blip in time.

There could be multiple reasons for accepting a more physically challenging lifetime. Balancing or releasing energies, as I have mentioned; and learning about *ourselves,* our inner strengths, through the challenges of a lifetime when it is necessary to face and overcome physical adversity.

Then there is the fact we often try to help in the teaching of each other; we may, for example, try to help another to learn more about compassion. So in our physical lifetime we present them with the opportunity to serve, as a helper, or our carer, for instance. The latter reason, to help teach others, also teaches us that the conditions we find ourselves in at birth may also have nothing to do with any personal karma.

Whether one believes in reincarnation and karma may seem unimportant if living a loving, caring and sharing life. Personally speaking though, I think it helps greatly to have a more comprehensive understanding of spiritual philosophy. Because one then gains a deeper, richer, more complete understanding of the interconnectedness of all life. This, encouraging respect for all life, whilst shining a new light on all the seeming inequalities we witness. Spiritual knowledge therefore helps us to make sense of life, and gives it greater meaning and purpose, and can only help us in our quest for spiritual progression.

To sum up this section:

- **The Soul (totality) – Is the real immortal Spirit Being. This can be called the Higher-Self – and always remains in the spirit realms.**

- **The Person on Earth – Is empowered by a percentage of the higher-self energies.**

- **Reincarnation – Is another physical lifetime empowered by a percentage of the energies of one's higher-self.**

- **Karma – Is the name given to soul energies that need to be rebalanced, or to be cleared or redressed either in spirit life or during another physical incarnation.**

12. Earth-bound and Lower Levels

On occasions those who pass-on can become "Earth-bound" as it is called. Meaning they remain in the immediate atmosphere of the Earth-plane rather than returning home to the spirit realms.

Such people illustrate the fact that life immediately after death is effectively an extension of the physical life.

More commonly, when someone passes-on they are met and guided towards the light of the spirit realms. However, for various reasons some refuse such help and remain close to the physical world.

Sometimes, particularly if a sudden or shock passing, this is because they immediately wish to see one or more of their loved ones on Earth. In fact they may not truly recognise that they have physically died, and may believe that they are dreaming. While in other cases, fear could cause them to reject assistance; for instance a fear of judgement.

Those who remain close to Earth, particularly if they have led any sort of selfish, cruel or embittered lives, may hold lower vibrational energies which have become part of their aura. Such people, and even those who have led quite harmless lives, may also retain what is sometimes called the "Vital" (or lower etheric) body which, under more normal circumstances, quickly dissolves when we return to spirit life.

By remaining attached to the Earth-plane with energies which are of a lower vibration such people can sometimes interfere with things on the material plane and on occasions may even be seen.

If they are malicious or mischievous they tend to be called, "Poltergeists". However, quite often any attachment to Earth is temporary and the personalities intend no harm and may, for example, simply move an object to draw attention to their presence because they wish to be recognised and to say goodbye.

Although there is no literal eternal hell, those who have led cruel or wicked lives may gravitate to lower less desirable hellish levels of the spirit realms until they show genuine remorse and seek to redress the results of their actions through service to others.

At these levels, measuring in Earth time, a personality aspect may remain 'trapped' because of their actions and by their thoughts and feelings, for a great many years.

I do not wish to dwell on this subject other than to say that such hell-like levels do exist. As those who have read *Escape from Hell* will realise.

Therefore (and sorry if this sounds like a sermon), it would be wise to live a life with respect shown to other people, to ourselves, and indeed to all life, animals and the environment, to ensure we are not drawn down to anywhere near such low vibratory levels.

13. Spirit Guides and Angels

Everyone has friends residing in the spirit realms. Quite often they belong to what is called our "Soul group". A group consists of like-minded souls on a similar vibration to each other, and may have been together in their spirit life for the equivalent of many thousands of Earth years. Members of the same soul group regularly undertake incarnations together in further excursions to Earth life.

On many occasions they are also born as members of the same family; or they may become a future partner, a husband or wife. An instant reciprocated attraction strongly suggests a pre-birth link. They may also swap roles from one incarnation to the next. So the father in one lifetime can become the son, the mother the daughter and so forth, and they are not limited to any one gender. (A previous lady-friend of mine was apparently my father back in Roman style times).

Occasionally we may return to the same physical family line as in a previous earthly lifetime. Especially if a child is 'lost' they may choose to return to the same mother or at least the same family. Many such cases are recorded in a book called, *Return from Heaven,* by Carol Bowman.

However, more generally when a link in one earthly family has reached a more natural and satisfactory conclusion, I understand that it is far more common to incarnate elsewhere. This could be in any country, dependent upon the needs and desires of the soul.

As well as role swapping (remember, to the higher-self they are all acting assignments with spiritual purpose) a member of the same soul group who has not incarnated may act as a guide to another. Although a guide from a higher level of the spirit realms will I am sure be attached to each soul group and may be its main guide.

When possible, those above in spirit life are always happy to help those below; and this principle and practice, of cooperation and guidance, extends from the highest levels downwards and all the way to Earth.

The role of spirit guides is to oversee and help guide our lifetime upon Earth. When we sleep our spirit form can temporarily leave the physical body, although retaining a link with it via what is called the "Silver cord" until 'death' when it snaps.

When the spirit travels during sleep this is called, "astral projection" or "astral travel", we may do so to discuss with our guide how our life in physical form is progressing or simply to meet-up with friends and loved ones who are already in spirit life. Although, and unfortunately, we rarely remember such excursions when we wake, or perhaps retain a snippet of recollection which we think of as a dream.

Our guide will also attempt to prompt our earthly minds, feeding us with thoughts and ideas intended to direct us upon our higher-self chosen pathway.

However, free-will enables us to accept or reject whatever thoughts manage to reach our physical consciousness.

We may hear someone say that they had a 'silly' thought or 'idea' pop into their head, and they dismiss it as the workings of their own imagination. Little do they realise that it may be a suggestion from their spirit guide or from their own higher-self. I wonder how many unscrupulous business people receive such a prompt that attempts to touch their conscience, and yet choose to ignore it?

Angels are spirit beings who work in numerous ways. There are angels who oversee the development of lower life forms, for example with nature, the trees, plants and flowers and so forth. Those who work with us are often called guardian or healing angels.

Basically, angels are spirit beings considered by some to follow a different line of evolution to ourselves. They, like any higher evolved souls, should not be worshipped. Like us, they are gradually progressing to higher levels of expression.

Under the direction of the Angels, nature spirits, fairies, pixies and gnomes (etc.) truly do exist, and they work with nature.

Angels and nature spirits are mentioned in various books, a couple from the White Eagle range on this subject are lovely to read and they are titled: *Spiritual Unfoldment II* and *Walking with the Angels*.

Nature spirits were also mentioned by Frédéric Chopin speaking from the spirit world by direct voice during a Leslie Flint sitting. The extract that mentions this is on

YouTube under the title: "Chopin Describes Fairies at his Valldemossa Garden".

On the recording Chopin is talking to the sitter Rose Creet about his small garden at Valldemossa on the island of Majorca and how nature spirits, or fairies, visited him there while he was composing.

As well as via YouTube many recordings of Chopin can be accessed on the Leslie Flint Educational Trust website: https://www.leslieflint.com/frederic-chopin

14. The Past, Present and Future

Spirit energy, which empowers each of us, has *always* existed. It is eternal and indestructible. However, energy has no individual consciousness or soul and mind unless this is developed. On Earth this happens gradually via lower life forms.

Therefore, ever so slowly in the long distant past, the energy that now empowers each human being and our higher-self, developed to the individualised expression that humans have reached through countless lower forms of expression.

These can include such as the mineral, plant, insect and animal kingdoms and may be spread over aeons of time. However, our development could have taken place on other planets and absolutely anywhere in this or another universe.

This is quite a mindboggling concept and teaching to grasp and imagine, especially the timescales, perhaps? Although, intellectually, this is in no way vital information to recognise and 'take on board' because this is all in 'our' past. Indeed, "our" may not even be a fair word to use? Because at these earlier stages the energy that today we would consider our own individualised energy, had yet to become "us".

Rudimentary, or undeveloped consciousness and spirit-mind energy develops, grows or expands to absorb and become greater and better able to grasp different concepts and ultimately love and deeper emotions. This, as I have said, happens gradually through a chain of progressively higher forms, each a little further along the chain, and last in this line of evolution before human are certain animals, principally, it was at one time said to be the domesticated Cat, Dog, Horse and Elephant. Whether any other animals can these days be added to this list we might ourselves (in spirit life) one-day discover. There may, I suspect, be isolated circumstances when an animal of another species might become sufficiently advanced by human contact and love to enable him or her to take this next step 'up the ladder' of evolution?

This is so because once mind energy has progressed sufficiently through the last link in the chain it then reaches a suitable level of vibration to effectively be 'born' in the spirit realms as an individualised soul. We usually call ourselves "individualised human souls", yet in reality we are *not* human, we are far, far greater, we are only human at this present moment in eternal life.

Before individualisation to the 'human' level of expression, at the animal stage and below, a group soul and mind is shared. At that stage all progress is naturally 'pooled' and shared by all in the same soul group.

In spirit life, we too, quite often share our energies and experiences and understanding with fellow souls from our own soul group and others. However, as individualised souls, we have a choice in this, so we could refuse to do so if we so wished or felt we had reason to say no.

When a soul first 'awakens' in spirit life at the individualised level of expression I understand that it generally (if ever) holds no memories of the lower level forms used for development of mind. It is effectively a 'new-born' soul. Although, that said, I have recently heard one report that suggests that a soul can access such memories – but I am yet to find confirmation of this.

Whether the absence of past memories is simply because the higher consciousness attained or reached at the individualised level is unable, and has no reason, to attune itself to a lower degree of mind, or whether the past is deliberately closed-off by some higher power, I am uncertain.

Perhaps a lack of past memory at this time is just as well? Let's face it, if we were to remember a previous lifetime in a different gender this would be confusing enough for us, but it would be a doddle compared to remembering being who knows what animal and lesser forms during 'our' history.

***

In most cases, unless purely to help another soul, the main purpose of our present lifetimes are to help each of us to quicken or increase our own soul vibrations. As we do so we are enabled to climb the spirit ladder of evolution as more enlightened spirit beings.

As I have previously mentioned, in spirit life before birth we do plan certain events and situations and relationships that we then encounter in physical life. The object is to take any opportunity planned, when it presents itself, and this may be to help clear or balance karmic energies. Alternatively, we may find ourselves undertaking experiences, or lessons as they are often called, we feel will further our spiritual progress.

Lessons are often incorporated in experiences that involve contrasts, love and hate, light and dark, good and bad, right and wrong, being rich and being poor, knowing freedom and its lack, and many more we cannot encounter in the spirit realms where all is in harmony on each level of vibration.

Many experiences can only be encountered upon a planet such as Earth. When we accept and successfully deal with the challenges we encounter, we grow spiritually.

Not everything that happens to us on Earth is pre-planned. In fact, comparatively very little is. We also have free-will; so even when a pre-planned opportunity comes along we are able to do as we please. So we certainly can stray from our intended plan. Our higher-self and our spirit guides will naturally try to impress upon us the desire to proceed as may have been planned, but how many free-will earthly decisions ignore the inner promptings? Some people, unfortunately, stray further than others.

***

As for our future, we have both an initial and a long-term future following our physical lifetime.

Assuming we, the earthly personality, have been of reasonably average behaviour in our current lifetime we will quickly progress to the astral level of the spirit world.

There, we can meet and reside with our loved ones and friends in a beautiful harmonious environment. We may be satisfied to remain at this level for some considerable time?

However, in the long-term future we will awaken to the reality of our higher-self. Then, as I said earlier, if we eventually have no need of the personality form we will initially have been using on the astral level, we will once more live and express ourselves from the perspective of our higher-self. None of this should be considered a scary or frightening prospect. We will not be losing ourselves. It will be natural and can only happen when we are ready and have awakened to a higher level of awareness.

Our future then, if we so choose and need, will be to undertake further physical lifetimes. Alternatively, if we have progressed sufficiently to no longer require or need to return to physical life we may, for instance, choose to train and become a spirit guide to others less progressed in the spirit world or upon Earth. Or perhaps we may choose to undertake service in some other capacity? Perhaps helping or rescuing those in lower levels of spirit life? Or working with newly arrived children or animals? There are countless opportunities and possibilities we can choose from and naturally, since we are free spirits, it is entirely up to us to do as we please.

Our future could, of course, be expressed anywhere in the universe and if we so choose in any form of a suitable vibratory level. We are told that many planets are inhabited by life-forms of an equivalent or higher level of development and expression than the human. Also, that other universes exist, and this highlights the never-ending adventures through time and space that may await each of us in the future.

In a sense we are all time travellers, just like Dr Who, as I explain in my book, *Adventures in Time and Space.*

64

Part Two:

Be Thyself

Introduction to Part Two

My friends, my intention in part two of this book is to encourage every reader, in all that they say and do in their physical life on Earth, to more genuinely, honestly and completely *be true to the real inner person they are*.

Most people probably think that they are already living exactly how they choose?

But many people do not; at least not fully. They are pushed and pulled, manipulated or coerced in various ways to behave and live in ways that do not reflect their real true inner self.

Some of the ways people are coerced may seem fairly harmless, yet even these can prove disempowering.

As well as having its serious side, I hope readers enjoy this part of the book, and even find it amusing in places?

Humour, and having a good sense of humour, *is* important. We need to have the ability to laugh at life and at ourselves at least some of the time, and not to take life too seriously.

After all, life *is* eternal. We *are* immortal spirit beings. Life on Earth is an adventure, so if we can have a laugh and hurt no one deliberately we will have the last laugh.

Laughter is therapeutic; it is literally good for one's health. I checked this out on the Internet and found that laughter is said to relax the whole body and relieve physical tension. It boosts the immune system, decreases stress, and releases endorphins which promote an overall sense of wellbeing.

So, laugh at my comments by all means, this is fine by me!

However, more seriously, I believe that it is important that we do not allow others too much sway over our decisions. We need to retain our own sovereignty, and truly be the free spirit who chooses exactly how we live; and especially we should never be fearful of being, saying and doing what we feel inwardly comfortable with.

If we don't remain totally true to our inner voice and conscience, if we allow others to push and pull us as they please, even if this is not deliberate on their part, we will to some degree at least be one of society's sheep.

By the way, I use the sheep analogy quite a bit herein, and it is not intended as an insult to anyone. I recognise the fact that we all follow the herd or flock mentality from time to time. We go with the crowd and enjoy the company. Sometimes it simply makes life easier and more fun, and more often harms no one.

However, this isn't always the case, because if we allow others too much say, too much power, this disempowering of self can be bad for self-esteem and confidence; it can even be bad for our health. It can also lead us off the pathway our higher-self may wish us to follow.

The spirit guide Silver Birch said fear was unnecessary. He wasn't suggesting we dismiss all reasonable commonsense, but how many of us allow some degree of fear to sway our decisions and what we say and do?

The following is what Silver Birch said about fear, and this is taken from one of many books of his teachings, titled: *Silver Birch Anthology.*

Fear is Unnecessary

'It is the relic of the days of early evolution when primitive man did not understand the processes of nature and attributed to them powers that were beyond the natural. He was afraid of the night; he was afraid of the sun; he was afraid of the storm, the lightning and the thunder; he was afraid of the tempest; he was afraid of all natural phenomena because the explanation of them did not come within his mental orbit.

'But you are no longer children of a primitive era. You boast that you are highly civilised, that you have grown to man's full, proud estate. Why, then, should you have fear, knowing that you are part of the Great Spirit of all life, that you are co-sharers in the processes of evolution, that you possess the power which shaped the whole universe and gave it direction and purpose, that you possess the power that is responsible for every facet of life, the power that filled the whole of the world with all that it contains? Why is fear essential when you know what you are and can be? No, fear is wrong, for fear makes you afraid and you should not be afraid. You should live in the sunlight of knowledge based on the confidence that you are infinite spirits and nothing can hurt or damage for ever the eternity which is yours.'

'NEVER allow fear to find a lodgement within your being. It is a negative quality, which destroys, vitiates and saps. It impairs your judgement; it clouds your reason; it prevents you from seeing issues clearly. There is no problem that comes to any soul, which you are incapable of solving. There is no difficulty that you cannot conquer - if you would but allow the latent divinity to rise to the surface.'

A prime example of how one's fear can have extremely detrimental effects is the Anita Moorjani story, as related in her excellent book, *Dying to be Me*.

In her book Anita relates how her cancer took her to the very brink of 'death'. To a near death experience (NDE) that revealed to her that *fear* was the primary reason for the cancer. She admits that prior to her NDE she was fearful of "*just about everything*". Of being disliked, of letting people down, of not being good enough, of illness. She says that she was basically "*afraid of living*", and "*terrified of dying*".

It was by eliminating fear and embracing greater self-love and of course much more that is detailed in her book, that the cancer was enabled to completely leave her physical body.

This is a major example of why we need to be true to ourselves, and not to allow other people to dominate us, or any degree of fear to prevent us from living according to our own agenda.

In my opinion, to be totally true to ourselves, it *is* necessary to be a genuine freethinker. I expect most people will agree with this? But how many of us are?

The flock mentality inhibits many people from thinking freely for themselves; consequentially, they behave and respond according to the dictates of their "programming".

Some programming is of course very, very difficult to overcome; and this is especially so if it originated in childhood. This is a fact known since ancient times, and the Greek philosopher, *Aristotle* is famously quoted for saying, '*Give me a child until he is 7 and I will show you the man.*'

However, if we can begin to recognise that it is present within ourselves, this allows for the possibility of our overcoming and eliminating the programming. Then our choices may more naturally come from our heart and soul, and follow the inner guidance of our intuition and conscience?

Shortly I shall begin to present some of my observations on "sheep like" behaviour. Readers may recognise some of these in themselves and in other people, and think of other examples? These centre on things that so many people allow themselves to blindly accept.

Some of the subject matter I include readers may, perhaps, consider rather trivial? Yet even with these seemingly "little things", in my opinion, many people are adhering to some degree of programming.

One should consider the strong possibility that, if they cannot be true to themselves with the little trivial things, what hope do they have with anything that really does matter?

Surely, if truly a freethinker, one must apply the results of their free thoughts to everything that they say and do?

This is what I am trying to encourage; for people to think more deeply about the choices they make, or accept. For instance, in regard to religion, as my earlier inclusion of the Menno quote hopefully made clear. He said what I totally agree with:

> *'Face up to life -* **study yourself** *- know where your faults lie and study them. Don't shrug your shoulders, and think of something which seems more pleasant to you'.*

In this way anyone can find out what it is that evokes their responses to make the decisions they do in life; and why.

In a way, I want readers to become their own psychoanalyst. Then to feel the guidance of their real inner self, the soul, rather than that of the physical personality (the ego) that has largely been shaped by upbringing and society in general.

This I endeavoured to do myself, many years ago while I lay quietly upon my bed, and I think it is something we need to do on a regular basis because it is very easy to slip into old habits!

Perhaps I should call it an inner search for honesty, *"are my motives really honourable or just a way of boosting my own self esteem?"* We all need to ask ourselves such questions at a deeper level of our being.

When we can do this and answer honestly, we truly will have found liberation, and freedom from the flock mentality (I'm on the sheep theme again); and we can more genuinely be true to ourselves.

It is in all aspects of life that we need to question ourselves; at least this is what I believe. If we discover that we have in any way been living according to the flock mentality, it is about time we freed ourselves and gained mental and emotional liberation.

Society's shepherds, who effectively "program" us to behave as they see fit can be practically anyone. They include family; teachers; friends and work colleagues; employers; and even comedians. Add to this those responsible for media marketing; doctors; clergy; the government; and in the UK (so-called) royalty. (Readers may think of others to add to my list).

It isn't easy to free oneself from thought programming and perhaps the dictates of the ego that has developed around this, but, as I have said, recognition of it helps, it is a starting point.

I make no attempt to go to the same depths of the human psyche as someone such as Eckhart Tolle. What I am presenting and my comments are based upon my personal experiences and observations, together with an understanding of spirit philosophy.

What matters is whether readers derive any benefit from my comments. If it helps anyone in any way at all, I will be delighted.

I have one suggestion to start with. When any reader needs to make a decision that they are not immediately sure about, I suggest they try to mentally step outside of themselves and see the situation as their higher-self might.

When any of us manage to do this it goes a long way towards helping us to make an appropriate decision.

I wish every reader good luck.

Earth's Programmers:

15. Family

My friends, the first, and for most people, foremost authority figures and first indoctrinators are family, and principally, parents. So often they instruct their children to believe, behave and think as they do.

More often than not this is acceptable and can even be a good thing, and for the benefit of the child, but for some it goes too far.

Programming may include a particular political allegiance, or perhaps a father's passion revolves more around football and the child is "encouraged" to follow the same team. Either way, the effective indoctrination is often fully absorbed by the child.

I know of one father who dislikes cats for no good reason I can see. *"They 'go' on my lawn",* is a typical excuse many people make for their dislike. His child 'inherited' the same 'auto-response' to the degree that he was seen attempting to kick a neighbours frail old cat for absolutely no reason.

I have since seen that such actions are now a legal offence against the animal welfare act of 2006. Teletext news I saw during 2019 reported that a 15 year old had been arrested for a similar assault against a cat.

It is from such early childhood actions that many a psychopath has developed!

The mother initially seemed totally indifferent to the actions of her son despite her presence. This effectively exasperated the situation by more or less sending a signal to the boy that such behaviour was acceptable! It is not. Inwardly at least we all know that it is not; and karmic consequences will follow such actions unless the actions are in some way rebalanced by perhaps later kind and caring actions.

Then there are what I'll call "family occasions". I expect that we have all heard someone effectively indoctrinated say that they "have" to attend a family occasion such as a birthday party, an anniversary, or a wedding or even a funeral?

Many people obey the family dictates and attend such gatherings regardless of whether they would really rather be elsewhere.

If it is suggested to them that they don't have to attend they stare quizzically in disbelief at such a comment or suggestion and say something like, "But it is traditional, we always gather (for whatever the occasion is)".

The expectations of the family are more or less blindly obeyed by the well-groomed sheep. They fail to see that all other family members who attend such gatherings were equally well programmed with the same seemingly compulsory obligations ingrained into their collective psyche.

Consequently, in such families, occasions such as Christmas, or a funeral - and sometimes even of a distant member of the family, are always attended.

However, if one of the family members begins to awaken, and truly think independently for themselves and questions the family traditions, and in a sense seeks independence from the flock, they sometimes face repercussions and quite possibly a barrage of emotional blackmail that tries to get them to 'toe the family line'.

When a "black sheep" ignores emotional family blackmail, the remainder of the family flock can sometimes turn against the freethinking rebel, and may even ostracise them to some degree.

They effectively are labelled as the family renegade who has to be shunned or treated with contempt until they once again obey the dictates of the family.

If they don't eventually fall into line, they may forevermore be treated as the family "leper", who is cut adrift in one way or another.

If the family have any level of financial wealth they may even be disinherited!!

Such extremes are perhaps rare, but because indoctrinated programming can in some cases be so deeply ingrained at conscious and subconscious levels of mind, such things have really been known to happen.

Many a family have members, brothers and sisters, a father and a son, and so forth, who 'fall out', to say the least, and never speak or even lose all contact with each other for decades, and quite often over some disagreement that neither may remember!

What I am advocating herein is for everyone to be and remain at all times true their own inner (soul) self, and to be a freethinker. However, at the same time to never forget that we are all spirit beings, so we should never allow ourselves to get caught up in any degree of argument or conflict concerning our decisions.

When one follows a pathway that is contrary to other family members, and this equally applies in all cases, one should do so in a respectful loving way. If others do not understand why we are following a different pathway to themselves, this can calmly and politely be explained to them. In this way they too may learn.

I am sure that another outcome to any 'falling out' with other family members is that their example is welcomed by one or more other members. They too admit to being tired of the expectation to "toe the family line". The result is that before too long, the courage of the one freethinking "black sheep" is the inspiration that gives others the courage to grab their share of liberation, and a new era is born.

The "bottom-line" is to **be true to oneself**. To follow the intuitive guidance of one's higher-self and to do what this guides and inspires us to do. If it hurts someone's feelings because of their own ingrained programming or indoctrination this cannot be helped. It is for them to wake-up and free themselves, and respect the freedom of others.

As I have said, we should naturally be polite and respectful to each other. When necessary we can always say, "Sorry if this offends", but above all we **must** always be true to ourselves.

One example of a very common and more or less indoctrinated 'tradition' is the ritual of sending Christmas cards to each other. But why do people do this?

Personally, I stopped the yearly "madness" of sending cards to relatives and friends decades ago. Most of these people I never saw from one year to the next.

I realised that it was 'crazy' – I was mostly sending the cards to say, "I'm still alive and at this address". They were doing the same, so occasionally I'd get a card with an update on a person's new address.

I decided that if I wanted to stay in touch I'd endeavour to telephone them at least once a year. I did tell them of my decision in the final year I sent a card, and at this time also suggested that they likewise stopped sending a card to me. After a few years of some forgetting and sending me one, the cards ceased arriving. I haven't lost a single friend as a result. In fact, while some have followed my example, most who still send them to other people appreciate the fact that they now have one less to send.

When I have spoken of this with newer acquaintances, some have said that they send cards to those who send them cards! So the ritual is self-perpetuating. In some cases it even extends to people met on holiday and never seen again!

In the house in which I live as I write this, the first Christmas after we moved-in, a card arrived addressed to some previous occupants for whom we had no forwarding address. The card never gave an address of the sender, so we couldn't return it. This happened for several years in a row, which suggests that the sender and intended receivers had little or no real contact. The annual ritual was being pointlessly observed.

Years ago I looked up the history of mailing cards to each other and found it started in Victorian times, when a certain gentleman commissioned some cards to be printed. **This shows how one person can have a massive impact in this world.**

No doubt the family and friends of this gentleman copied the idea, and from there it "took off". Not that the poor in Victorian times would have had the funds to follow the trend. But gradually through the decades it was adopted.

So when someone says, "it's traditional to send cards", they can be informed that it is a practise that only began with the wealthier in Victorian days. It is amazing just how the poor sheep of society have so often followed the trends set by the wealthy.

Those who still send Christmas cards really should ask themselves why, and whether they truly want to do this or are simply following some ingrained expectations of others? It is of course a fairly harmless annual ritual and I have no desire to suggest that everyone who continues with it is adhering to inner programming. I mention it to encourage readers to not only consider what they may consider bigger issues in life, but to also give consideration to the seemingly little things. By considering everything, from minor to major, we become better attuned to our true inner self. If we do not give consideration to absolutely everything we think, say and do, we allow at least some degree of programming or the directives of others to lead us. If we do allow this, who knows where it will lead us? We are responsible either way.

I can continue with the "Christmas" theme and talk about Christmas gifts. I find it quite absurd how for some this escalates to cost more and more each year. This is another ritual I stopped, also decades ago in my case. It would I think be mean to exclude children, let them have some fun and excitement by all means, but do grown people need to "forever" worry about finding something for each other? This is especially sad if their finances are tight.

What I've said so far may seem comparatively minor 'indoctrinations', and those that happen in most families.

But there are more damaging families. Those who teach racial or colour hatred, or those who are homophobic or have zero respect for animals (as my earlier example with the aging cat demonstrated), or even everyday neighbours.

Such things can, unfortunately, be ingrained in the next generation and such cycles are hard to break.

Most people who read this book, thankfully, won't pass such traits along even if they witnessed them.

But there are a thousand little traits that can be taken within the psyche of children. The only way to uncover these is to constantly ask oneself questions, such as: "Why do I do the things I do, or think, or react in this or that way?"

The majority of traits may be harmless and quite neutral in effect on us and on others. But we may also find some that could be leading us in a way that is not in our higher interests. These, we can endeavour to change.

Before I leave behind the family programming, I have another question, and this one seems to apply amongst practically all family clans, "why do so many people still dress in depressing drab "mourning black" for a funeral?" Why do it? What is the point? What is the reason? Whose benefit is this supposedly for? "It is traditional", the sheepish will no doubt bleat in my direction.

Well, guess what, I checked this out and found that it dates back quite a way in some cultures, but not in all. White was even considered appropriate at one point in history! In the UK, wearing black mostly spread from the same Victorian times as the Christmas card habit. Queen Victoria wore black for 40 years after the death of her husband, and this was featured in magazines and, before long, it was copied by society's sheep.

It should be obvious to all that to wear black to a funeral holds no significance and serves no purpose. Therefore, when next attending a funeral, if one does, I suggest wearing any colour but black to be true to our inner self and wishes. Of course, some people simply like to wear black, regardless of the occasion. But otherwise, if we dress to please others, or simply because we don't want to look "different", or be the odd one out, this is being dishonest to oneself.

I'm sure that many people who attend the average funeral wish they had the nerve to wear any colour other than black. My suggestion is, "be the change". Be the trend setter, the one who rocks the boat, in the long run I believe we make more freethinking and genuine friends this way.

Many people's attitudes can be changed in response to the one who truly thinks and acts in a liberated way. This is beginning to happen in many families and groups already.

I'll share something personal, when my mother passed from the Earth life in 2006, I didn't mourn. I recognised that she would be well and happy in her return to life in the spirit realms. A small gathering of us, her relatives, had a natural woodland funeral for her. We didn't have any of the typical "official" services that so often accompanies such occasions.

In other words we didn't pay a vicar or some other member of the clergy, as some people do, to ask us questions about my mother and to take reference notes so that he or she could later talk about my mother at a service.

I expect most people have seen such services, when the clergy (who typically had never met the 'deceased') gives everyone present a life overview of the 'departed', and says how they will be missed. More or less, the clergy are a hired actor!!

At the Woodside burial site of my mother we each said whatever we fancied, and dressed how we wished. It was not disrespectful to anyone; my mother, not following any religion, would certainly not have wanted anyone to follow some meaningless ritual or tradition.

It was a hot summer's day. I wore shorts and a casual cotton shirt as is my normal attire for such a day. How many people would do likewise? That is, dress exactly how they might truly wish, despite any "disapproval" directed towards them from their indoctrinated family and friends? If any readers says, "yes" then I congratulate them. Because this shows that they may already be a free spirit.

Victoria is also responsible for why so many brides choose white for their wedding gown.

She went against the trend and did so in 1840 and this too was copied by society's sheep-like people. Before then, red was commonly the colour of choice, reflecting red roses, the symbolic flower of love.

This certainly won't be an issue for me, as a man, and an aging one at that. But seriously, as a non-royalist, as all freethinkers surely should be, bowing down to no one, do please inform young ladies who think they are being themselves that this may not be strictly so. They are following in the footsteps of Queen Victoria and countless other brides since. They are copying, even if inadvertently, as for nearing two hundred years so many others have copied.

However, and obviously, and one hundred percent, the choice is their own to make. I am merely encouraging everyone to think, and in this case dress, how they truly fancy regardless of what others think, and to be themselves rather than a sheepish follower.

16. Schools and Teachers

My friends, other authority figures who may take control over the developing minds of the young are school teachers.

In my opinion, in the UK, English and Mathematics are the sole two academic subjects that by necessity should be taught to children. We all need these to some degree at least.

However, even these are essential only to enable us to read and get by in life. If a child or student should wish to progress further, to write and express themselves in words, or to go into other fields that require a grasp of higher mathematics, then this should be their own decision to make.

Computing is today taught in schools, and no doubt this is appreciated by many children. It wasn't around when I was attending schools back in the 1950's and 1960's. Today many children seem to understand many aspects of this far more than the likes of me. No doubt many have been trained in this field in spirit life pre-birth, but this is a story for another time.

As for modern schooling, it seems to me that in some respects little change has occurred since my school days, when so many children were forced to sit at desks in stuffy box shaped rooms and stare forward at a teacher who much of the time was busy teaching utterly pointless information that totally bored most children.

From my point of view, knowing what I know these days, the single most important teachings that should be presented to every child are the genuine spirit facts of life; these include the law of karma.

Children would then have a far better understanding of what life was really all about. Personally, I think they would greatly appreciate learning about this. Ultimately, of course, it is the single most important aspect to everyone's life.

Subjects such as History and Geography are still included in the compulsory national curriculum.

In my opinion, the only History truly worth teaching to children is the bits we could learn from, such as how destructive and indiscriminate war has proven to be. And how numerous world religions have divided people and caused hatred and should be regarded as an insult to the intelligence we call God. If we taught these things we might find children growing-up with greater tolerance for other races and nations.

Geography surely has little if any value. This has proven especially so in recent times, when the country names and boundaries keep changing. If travelling abroad people simply get on a plane and leave it to the pilot to get them to their destination. Even he or she will engage "auto-pilot". The holiday tour operator's magazine may include a map to show people the flight route and the country's position on the globe, but few will even look at this.

The majority of people travel from the UK to countries where they are more likely guaranteed sunshine. Directions from the holiday accommodation to the local taverns are generally more appreciated than knowledge of where their destination lies on a global map. Internal travel sometimes only requires knowing where the right bus stop or train station is located. People with cars either look at a map or use a satellite navigation system.

The teaching of foreign languages can naturally be useful. If a pupil is capable and wishes to study and learn more than one language this ought to be encouraged.

In an ideal society a multiple choice of possible subjects should be available for students to select from, so that they can try those they feel attracted to, with no rules to say pick one and stick to it.

It should be appreciated that every individual child has different needs. This is why so many of them suffer and rebel at regimented schooling that teaches boring and often pointless subjects.

Any serious emphasis on school exams should also be ceased. All one needs are a few basic checks to make sure a child has a reasonable grasp of English to read and Mathematics to cope in life.

Parents first, but schools also, should definitely encourage social skills. These should include being polite, kind and honest, and respectful of others in a caring and loving way; and teach why these are virtues to be valued and admired. Together with the implications of unworthy behaviour upon one's own soul.

Students could also be encouraged to use energy in a positive, fun way. Relaxation and exercise options should be plentiful. Complementary subjects such as meditation and yoga ought to be included, as should song and dance.

But of course, if they *were* taught about the spiritual nature of life, communicative mediumship and spiritual healing could also be developed from an early age – because the reality of spirit life should in no way be feared or regarded as anything other than a valid subject for discussion and study. (The suppression of this awareness and the fear associated with spirit communication is directly related to the influences of the Christian church).

To these add some optional, practical skills, gardening and how to grow fruit and vegetables, cooking, carpentry, plumbing and other trades, and whatever else could be put on offer so that students could begin to learn pastimes or a trade they are good at and, importantly, enjoy.

In my opinion, people should find an occupation that they not only enjoy but also find fulfilling. I believe that this is of great importance, and would help to create a peaceful and well-balanced, integrated, society.

Presentations (or workshops) on each subject, and here I'll add in artistic and again musical pursuits, could offer the opportunity to view, evaluate and perhaps try each that appeals. People love music and beautiful art of all varieties so why not encourage such hobbies and possible careers? How about comedy for an option too?

In this way, people of the future could be drawn to a trade or profession and lifestyle that appeals, instinctively (or spiritually), intellectually and practically.

Schools should offer the opportunity to find out what suits the individual, rather than forcing them all to learn the same curriculum, so much of which becomes meaningless within a short period of time.

I am not against any subject provided the child or student wishes to pursue it. We will always need scientists, veterinarians, surgeons, doctors, nurses, dentists, and healers, nutritionists, archaeologists, university lecturers, police and prison officers, and an endless list of other professions. But children and students should be freer to follow their heart or their inner soul driven direction.

I remember some of the rubbish I was taught as a young child. Such as how many wives Henry the Eighth had. We were taught their names, and how they died – those beheaded – and other nonsense. There was even some rhyme to help children remember it all.

Unless one becomes a quiz contestant or champion where a question on this subject crops up, what is the point? History buffs may disagree, but this aspect of my schooling and most of the rest, has never served a single worthwhile purpose in my life to date.

The only "academic" things I learned at school that have served a purpose in my life were Mathematics and English. I am no "master" at either of these; but the basics have proven themselves of value to me.

I did also enjoy sports as a child.

One subject that no child should be forced to endure, as I was to some degree at least, is "religious education" (as they called it). My schooling didn't go to any extremes in this regard, unlike some schools that make a thorough job of indoctrination.

Religions, other than Spiritism and Spiritualism, are based on faith and old fables. So no one can genuinely be "educated" in religion – because there are no proven facts. They can only be "brainwashed" into accepting "beliefs" based upon "faith" presented as though they were true factual stories.

They may as well be taught that Cinderella and Peter Pan were real historic stories.

So, the bottom line is, those with children or grandchildren should recognise the absurdity of sending them into institutions that will "brainwash" them and may even dumb or destroy their creativity and imagination. Where they will be "controlled" and learn to "toe the line" and "obey orders". Where they will only be able to eat and drink when they are told they can; and can only visit the toilet with permission. Then, when they eventually leave, they will be encouraged to chase money and possessions with no concept of their origins as unique individualised spirit beings.

Instead of developing into young freethinking and caring and compassionate adults their heads will be full of memorised data that will do nothing other than prove they are capable of retaining this data (for a while at least).

They may end up with some university degree to boast about, and yet still from necessity find themselves serving customers in a branch of Wetherspoon or filling shelves in a Supermarket? When they could have learned that it was fine to be creative and do something they fully enjoyed.

I have no children. But if I did I would have much preferred to have taught them at home, or found a school that was centred on the principles I have presented.

If my thoughts resonate with anyone they may serve some good? Because when an idea gets "out there" in the world it can take on a life of its own and reach many minds. Like the single gentleman and the Christmas card. An idea can mushroom and have an impact and make a worldwide difference.

This is so because our spirit or soul nature is far, far more powerful than most people realise, and connected to all other souls and life in this universe and beyond.

I am delighted to note that "Home Schooling" is a growing trend and that more and more parents are taking this option!!

17. Friends and Work Colleagues

My friends, if it isn't enough that sheepish people follow the dictates of those they accept as authority figures, a great many also allow equally sheepish friends and work colleagues, to influence what they think, say and do.

Quite often it is those who shout the loudest who lead them. The sort of person who will try to ridicule or belittle others and get them to follow the "party line" for fear of appearing different. In such circles unless something is deemed "acceptable" to the collective or those dominant within, it isn't done. Effectively these indoctrinators are the grown-up school bullies!

One simple example of this is so-called fashion.

Not so long ago, and perhaps still so today, even children felt embarrassed if they didn't wear clothing and footwear with expensive brand labels. Training to fall into line and follow the leaders of the flock starts very young.

Another example is the wearing of socks with sandals. In years gone by, socks were worn for comfort and warmth, or to avoid sunburn and to prevent the sandals from rubbing the bare flesh. In other words it was a commonsense decision and no comment was deemed necessary.

But these days, the sheepish people have been so well indoctrinated by the self-proclaimed "fashion gurus" that they collectively bleat, "You can't wear socks with sandals".

Such people would rather be burnt or blistered and in pain than be "different" from the flock. Or worse, they may have tough feet and a good suntan and think everyone else should be like them and regardless of whether this would hurt them.

These people are more or less self-obsessed and they too have been well programmed.

As for the self-proclaimed fashion gurus, I have seen some examples of their ideas of what to wear presented on TV, and in many cases their ideas appear quite ridiculous.

The sole intention appears to be the desire to look "unique" or "different". Yet as soon as seen, if liked, mass production or imitation copies appear everywhere, and the wearers appear as yet another clone and any claim to be "different" is lost.

To follow any fashion "statement" is simply to join another flock.

Haircuts can be another example of the flock mentality. Many people copy the haircuts of so-called "celebrities". What sheep they are.

Likewise, the idea of drinking or smoking, or taking other "recreational" drugs and so forth because "everyone does it", is to be a very gullible sheep.

I find it quite appalling that so often so-called "celebrities" in films, on TV or on chat shows, 'joke' about highly damaging drugs like cocaine. Treating the

taking of such drugs like a bit of social 'fun' that we all do!! (Until too late!! In many cases).

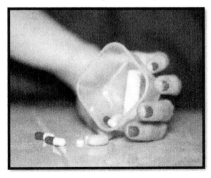

Then we also see those who are celebrated for going into rehab and hopefully overcoming their addiction. These people are not in any sense 'heroes' or to be admired unless they help to teach others of the dangers and damage that such drugs can cause. Otherwise, what are they teaching people? That it is 'fun' to take such drugs and then receive attention? People perhaps need to see more of the misery caused by such drugs to understand that joking about them is totally irresponsible and damaging to the physical person and the progression of the indwelling soul. **We are all each other's teachers!**

We all need to delve within, and "feel" what our inner motivation, our intuition, is saying to us, and follow its guidance. To recognise that there are those who seek to tie us to the flock mentality so that they can influence and direct our lives to fulfil their own agenda.

We need to raise our consciousness above the programming that abounds upon this planet and truly be freethinkers. To be people who recognise and know ourselves as spirit beings, and follow pathways that truly reflect our awareness.

18. Employers

My friends, I may be straying to a situation that we feel less able to easily take full charge of and to make changes. But here goes.

I'll start with a question for every reader to consider: "**There is a minimum wage, so why is there no maximum wage?**"

I believe that it is morally deplorable that those such as company "directors" or "executives" receive remuneration that is comparatively astronomical in comparison to the average employee.

Personally, I'd set a maximum wage at no more than three times the minimum wage, if not less, to help create a fairer, more equal society. I used to say ten times, but I've come to feel that this is too much of a discrepancy between the higher and lower paid. With this and everything I say, readers may have their own opinions on what would be justifiable and sensible?

After all, would any director or executive want to sweep the streets, empty the bins, care for the incapacitated and incontinent, or stack the shelves of supermarkets or one of countless other jobs that need to be undertaken? *No they would not.*

All inequalities that exist in society need to be challenged. Collectively we have the power to change anything we wish to change, please do recognise this

because it is a fact. We simply need enough of us to spiritually wake up.

Another example of those people who are being paid extreme salaries is top rated footballers and the like. Salaries at the top level are now obscene.

Football used to be a bit of fun; if we look back far enough in history it was a fact that some players used to travel on the same bus to a match as the supporters.

Ticket prices and TV subscriptions would be a fraction of the price if the greed was removed. It is the indoctrinated sheepish people who allow this and who can change this by refusing to pay.

There are no easy answers when it comes to employers. To argue with them can be at personal cost, and trade unions have lost much of the power they briefly enjoyed.

I simply hope that one day, when spiritual knowledge becomes more recognised, ethical and fair employers who organise more cooperative policies will develop and become the norm.

As people gradually become more enlightened and stop following the flock mentality perhaps they will start supporting the traders who are cooperatives, and then the empires of the greedy retailers will crumble or likewise change.

I'll emphasise again that collectively we have the power in our hands to change so much; it just needs the spark of recognition to reach sufficient numbers of people.

All this starts with the self. If we need to change and can find it within ourselves to do so, to better express our true inner selves upon Earth, others will follow our example. The example of the one, then the few, can help to generate a ripple effect that can spread far and wide and eventually bring an awakening and a new way of life that can benefit the many.

All we need do is *be the change* and not let old habits and conditioning rule us.

19. Comedians

Many sheepish people have their "adopted shepherds". In some cases this includes comedians who appear in theatres or on TV.

The comedian may say something which is "funny", for instance, about spirits, ghosts or the afterlife; or derogatory about mediums. What they say will get a laugh, and suddenly the subject and all who work in this field are to some easily led people fit only for ridicule.

If this stayed within the confines of a theatre or TV comedy routine this would, perhaps, be of lesser concern. However, it doesn't; it gets into the collective psyche of many of the gullible sheepish members of society. Consequently, they assume that all mediums, including the most honourable and genuine, are frauds or deluded individuals.

Anyone who dares to utter a word in defence of the accused people or subject is laughed at by all in the flock. The little voice in the head may say, "But I know there are genuine mediums and life beyond the physical", but this is kept quiet because freethinking is not permitted in the flock. They feel that they must, "follow the pathway of obedience or be ostracised".

What follows the death of the physical form really should be the very first question that any sensible freethinking person seeks to answer. Anyone who doesn't want to answer this is, to my way of thinking,

rather odd. After all, it has to make a massive impact upon how we view and live our lives.

Awareness that there is a "life after death" in isolation to all other spirit understanding may not change how anyone conducts their life. However, when more knowledge is added, and an understanding of spirit laws, those enlightened do become far more inclined to live respectful lives.

I am in no way suggesting that everyone who lacks spirit understanding is less than decent. There are of course millions of very nice people who have little spirit life awareness. However, when we live in the dark we are far more likely to make regrettable choices, and this is why I would absolutely love to see more people become aware of their true spirit nature.

Those who are too frightened to investigate the truth for themselves, and seek to verbally intimidate others from seeking answers, as may be the case with some comedians, are in many ways rather cowardly.

It probably seems much easier for a comedian or anyone else to jump on the bandwagon of ridicule, to scornfully poke fun at mediums and those who accept the genuine factual truth that life *is* eternal, than to seek answers for themselves. However, unless they do one day investigate, they will forgo the pleasure and delight of discovering the truth about their own true spirit self.

Perhaps they are too busy trying to have "fun" to face the subject? There is nothing wrong with enjoying a laugh, in fact, and as I have said, it is good for us. I cannot blame them for wanting to enjoy life and raise spirits through humour; in fact I applaud them for doing so.

The catch twenty-two of this is that I don't go much on political correctness, so why shouldn't they laugh at mediums, some are funny.

The most damaging problem arises when the ingrained belief system of a comedian causes them to present their opinions as though they were facts. They are not; they are prejudiced views based on speculation and misinformation and in some cases outright lies.

In regards to outright lies, the Wikipedia website is utterly unreliable in regard to the genuine spiritual nature of life and information in regard to a number (and there have been very many) of scientists who accepted the overwhelming evidence for the 'afterlife', as it is so often termed.

Whereas, one website where many of these top scientists are accurately reported is that of Victor Zammit who, together with his wife, Wendy, produced the book, *A Lawyer Presents the Evidence for the Afterlife.* The website is listed in the appropriate section near the end of this book.

Continuing with the subject of comedians:

A comedian may deliver a humorous "judgement" (about mediums or spirits - 'ghosts' as they may term them) that becomes amplified by audience laughter and applause which for some people only reinforces the mind-set that tells them what to think. In this case it is to believe an absolutely incorrect view of the true nature of life. This certainly isn't funny because, as I have more or less said before, when we live in ignorance we are far more likely to do ignorant things that, in time, will bring repercussions that will impact upon our spirit future. **The warning is all too clear in my book,** *Escape from Hell.*

We should make every effort to never allow anyone to lead or mislead us. While we should endeavour to always be and remain a freethinker and investigate everything important in life thoroughly for ourselves. In this way we can be true to our own higher-self.

One such 'comedian' and comedy actor 'guilty' of misleading others (although it is the personal responsibly of each of us to do our own research) is held in high esteem and seems to be considered as 'highly intelligent' and knowledgeable on a range of subjects. Some people consequentially allow themselves to believe that he must be right and know what he is talking about when he openly, and quite wrongly, says that there is no afterlife. I have seen at least three other 'comedians' say the same thing no doubt after accepting what the other 'comic' said!! However, readers should be aware that 'academics' and the like are often very, very closed-minded. They so often do perpetuate falsehoods based on their own faulty education. Be warned!!

20. Media Marketing

My friends, media marketing, the sort that wants customers to buy the products they are promoting, are quite successful at persuading people to purchase all sorts of things.

"Advertising pays" is an established fact. People often buy an advertised brand rather than a product with no brand name.

This applies to most common products, whether it is packaged foods for humans, for cats or dogs, washing powders or liquids, shampoo and practically every other item on an average shopping list. Then there are more expensive items such as cars; and quite disgracefully, in my opinion, advertisements that encourage people to gamble.

With the latter, if we pay attention we notice how it is more often than not young men supposedly, "having a good time". The commercial may even show a gambler "checking out" at a certain stage of a football match with winnings. They almost never show the truth; that most gamblers lose, and lives can be ruined to the point of desperation and even suicide. Advertisements keep being shown because bookmakers always make money from the manipulated gullible sheep.

As for the household purchases, mostly we may think of advertisements as harmless. We regularly need certain things anyway. Yet marketing "programming" seeps into the psyche and influences behaviour in so many ways.

It no longer seems acceptable to move home and inherit an "adequate" kitchen with ample units. The self-styled "experts" say, "Rip it out and put in a new kitchen". When did this become such a necessity? I'm quite sure that not so long ago people simply accepted what they found, gave them a clean, and got on with life. So often these days a new kitchen is for show.

The media convince people that they should have a "show home" in appearance, and the gullible and ego trained sheepish people go along with it. They then invite family and friends along so that they can show off. Others do the same thing with the latest technology; it used to be called "keeping up with the Jones's".

Media advertising is an attempt at mind manipulation; it coerces so many gullible people away from being true to their inner and unique self. Instead they become the person the media tell them they should be. The programming which more or less is brainwashing is so successfully ingrained that most people do not recognise it, and believe they are happy to live and be as they are directed. At least until something traumatic happens in their life. It is little wonder that so many people are experiencing a NDE. We need something to wake people up to their true nature.

Media marketing may seem an innocuous and harmless subject? However, it is a tool of the spiritually ignorant and greedy that directly or indirectly encourages people to accept the material world as the sole reality. It effectively suggests to people that they should place income and possessions at the top of their priority list. Consequently, so many people will sadly struggle to really be true to their inner soul or even to recognise themselves as a spirit being.

These are facts that really *should* be broadcast worldwide!

21. Doctors and Drugs

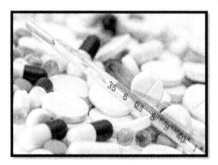

My friends, many people do whatever their doctor tells them to do without question or query.

The doctor may say, "Take two of these, three times a day after meals for a fortnight, and we'll see how we go." Adding, "If they don't do the trick, we'll try something else", and the patient does as instructed without questioning the experiment – with side effects - that is going to take place on their physical body.

At the same time, if asked for their opinion about the possible benefits of any alternative or complementary therapy, the average doctor will generally dismiss the subject as "untested", or placebo at best.

Basically, the majority of them seem to give little support or encouragement to any patient who may be willing to try a complementary or self-help route.

Most people seem to overlook the fact that the doctor's prescription and, "We'll see how we go", is nothing but a chemical experiment upon their patient.

Although I am sure that quite a few doctors do have awareness of the composite whole of mind, body, and spirit, it seems the majority do not. Consequently, it seems to me that many doctors seek to help a condition in isolation to its cause.

It should be obvious to everyone that if a root cause remains untreated, it is akin to putting out a fire in one room without tracing and fixing the faulty wiring that started it.

It seems that there are still a great many doctors, happy and willing to ridicule complementary therapies or treatments. Does medical training tell them that they can't work? In the same way that it seems many scientists are wrongly taught that spirit communication is a lie?

Homeopathy, herbal or flower remedies, and all similar treatments including the use of colour and crystals, spirit healing and Reiki, are attempts to harmonise the composite whole of mind, body and spirit. We are spirit beings and spirit guides do teach us that disease (or disharmony) appears first in the aura and if left untreated can proceed to materialise in the physical body.

Like orthodox medicine, complementary therapies or treatments are still limited if the root cause of the initial disharmony (or imbalance) remains unresolved. But they can and very often do help – and unlike many drugs, they should cause no adverse side effects.

The average doctor may well shout, "Placebo", or say, "It is a coincidence when a patient improves after having a complementary treatment or therapy".

They could of course say the same thing about their own prescription drugs; and they *do* sometimes give patients a placebo prescription during their own drug trials.

The physical body is a self-regulating mechanism that when treated with care and respect *is* capable of healing itself of almost any disease or disharmony. Especially if the mind is free from harmful emotions, such as fear, as the Anita Moorjani case mentioned earlier demonstrates.

If on the other hand someone holds any negative thoughts that carry any degree of hatred or resentment, or feels unable to offer forgiveness, or for some reason cannot love their own self and express their self as they might wish, then such negative emotions can be reflected in the aura and ultimately prove very harmful to the physical body.

Another thing I wonder is why Arthritis advice is not freely given to everyone who even vaguely develops the symptoms? In my experience it seems that in the UK most doctors fail to tell people that diet can make a huge difference. In many cases, all one need do is to cut back on "acid" foods and drinks. Information on which foods and drinks are acid or alkaline can be found online.

One cannot really be true to their higher-self unless they are willing to take personal responsibility for every aspect of their life. Naturally we all need some help and advice at times, for no one can be an expert on everything. We are also here on Earth to be each other's teachers.

Life can also be stressful and emotional at times.

We are here to experience, none of us live perfect lives all the time; we all err.

If we were sufficiently advanced in our soul energies we probably would not be here in our physical bodies. We would have evolved beyond the need to be here. We should therefore be gentle on ourselves because we can only do our best from one moment to the next. If we spot our own weaknesses, then this gives us the opportunity to spiritually grow by eliminating them, as best we can.

My advice, always, is to take control and allow no person, no matter their status or title, to direct how we live. If someone suggests something then it is entirely our choice as to whether we follow this suggestion or advice or reject it.

Above all, keep smiling, and remember, as *Carly Simon* sang, *Life is eternal.*

22. The Clergy

My friends, if the religion of the family is not football or some other sport, or they are not agnostics or atheists, the clergy may ensnare the poor flock.

The chief "indoctrinator" into a religion may be a priest, vicar, rabbi, mullah, or some other "holy man" (authority) figure. They will instruct the young lambs in the rules of the particular religion into which they have been born.

Indoctrination begins at an early age, when the young earthly mind is more impressionable (the first seven years, remember). The child is told that they are a Christian, Jew, Hindu, Muslim, or whatever, and expected to live and behave as one.

The child dare not question whatever the indoctrinator tells them, or in extreme cases, does to them.

The Roman Catholic Church is riddled with a history of priests who have abused young children, and principally boys. What part do the parents play in complicity? Why do they place their trust in such authority figures?

Men who dress in what is basically "fancy dress" and supposedly are so "pure" they never allow themselves the pleasure of a sexual partner – or so they claim. In reality of course many are gay (homosexual) men who, historically at least, have tried to hide their sexuality from the world.

There is of course nothing wrong with being gay, and the vast majority of gay people would never abuse a child in any way. Furthermore, many excellent entertainers and actors can be counted amongst those that are openly gay. It's about time the Catholic Church dropped the pretence and absurdity of pretending their clergy are any different to other people.

One can only conclude that the brainwashing of parents was a complete "success"? Otherwise they would surely never allow such men, who in some (and all too many) cases have turned out to be paedophiles, the opportunity to have free and especially private, access to their children. Like psychopaths and sociopaths they can appear charming and likeable on the surface, but inwardly they are ruthless predators.

Some religions are even more ruthless; and the growing child may develop into such a well-programmed sheep that eventually they will willingly carry explosives and die a so-called martyr's death for their faith. I have a quote in my book, *Golden Enlightenment-Twenty Year Anniversary Edition* that speaks of what befalls such easily manipulated people.

In the UK we have "Remembrance Day" – a couple of minutes officially on November 11th at eleven o'clock in the morning when people are encouraged to remember those who lost their physical lives in conflict or war.

This more or less seems another religious ritual when everyone stands in silence or silent prayer, with old soldiers in uniform prominent at many gatherings. (How do they keep getting those uniforms to fit? Or do they have new versions made?).

But why do the sheep of society bother with such a ritual? Why also do so many people keep bleating on about the great sacrifice fallen soldiers, sailors and air force personnel made?

Of course, they may well have been brave people. But either the people who keep performing the yearly ritual believe that those physically perished have ceased to be, and if people believe that, as many do, who are they praying for or trying to show respect to?

Whereas, those who accept or know the true facts, and that there *is* a spirit world, must surely realise that the "fallen" have "got up" in spirit and are NOT dead. So they don't need the ritual, the respect or admiration or whatever the reason why so many people keep this up.

I am sure that those who have "lost" someone in circumstances that from a physical perspective might be considered "prematurely", already think of them more or less every day, they are never forgotten, and don't need set times of remembrance.

Those who have 'died' (under any circumstances) can receive thoughts of love from those of us upon Earth on any day and at any time of day or night. Visits to graveyards to remember or talk to someone in spirit life are equally unnecessary. They are not in a grave or in any way tied to their former physical body, no more than they are tied to an old coat that they have discarded.

In my opinion, any religion that understands the truth of spirit life should distance themselves from these meaningless rituals. But the fact is that most religions do not understand because they are stuck in the dogma of their past history.

One thing is for certain; those who embrace any religion will never truly be free. Never will they truly, "Be thyself". They cannot, if they follow any religion – any belief system. Because it is "belief" ONLY that all religions are based upon!!

Readers with an interest in the subject of religion may find my book: *Christianity: The Sad and Shameful Truth*, worth reading.

23. Spiritualists and New-Agers

Sheep-like behaviour, or following the directives of an organisation, isn't limited solely to the average person or, for instance, those who follow an orthodox religion.

Many Spiritualists complain that their "movement" now has rules that impose party-line directives upon the mediums and committees.

Many mediums say that they are obliged to fall into line and follow the rules or dictates imposed. Their alternative is to be dropped and unable to demonstrate within the established outlets (churches and centres).

To degree, they are disempowered from communicating or teaching to the public exactly how they and their spirit guides might wish. They must work within constraints and follow the rules; otherwise they may not work at all. I'm sure that many feel obliged to toe-the-line. I can understand their dilemma, and do not suggest they all leave. It is perhaps better to be able to work with some constraints than not to work at all. But I think it would perhaps be wise for them to think deeply and move forward according to their intuitive guidance.

I hope that this book will encourage some mediums to consider any possibility to speak out against rules that they feel are unfair. Especially against rules that deny the medium the right to deliver communications and teachings appropriate to the guidance coming through from their spirit guides. Although I must also say that organisations do require some rules and guidelines because otherwise they open themselves to mediums delivering teachings that conflict with their own.

I judge no one. What I am encouraging is for everyone to follow and do as their heart and conscience dictates – as I'm sure most do.

Those who endeavour to follow a more ancient or "Pagan" tradition that embraces nature, the sun or constellations, and which rather paradoxically are often called "New Age", are more natural than the orthodox religions, such as Christianity. Yet even here I observe considerable sheep-like behaviour.

Some "new age" sheep seem to believe practically anything. Some teachings say, "Think like this and everything desired will be forthcoming".

Invariably, when people "want" something, if they cannot simply get this by purchasing it, some will eventually find they get what they want, while others will not.

Those who do not get what they wished for sometimes end-up feeling unworthy, or that they were doing something wrongly. They may be told by others, "You didn't believe it deeply enough, otherwise it would have worked".

What twaddle (rubbish) this is.

This is no different from the so-called faith healer who claims to heal in the name of God, and if someone doesn't get well, they say that it is because the person had insufficient faith, or because this was God's will.

This is twaddle of the cruellest kind.

The purpose of life, *The Reason Why You Were Born* (as I titled a previous book), is for spiritual growth, to increase one's soul awareness and vibration in order to progress to higher levels of spirit expression.

This, as I am sure I have said in part one, happens gradually as we undertake many lifetimes and experiences which enable a greater appreciation to be absorbed within the soul energies.

Effectively, we are actors who, through many incarnations, need and choose to play an array of parts to gain sufficient wisdom to climb further up the ladder of spirit progression.

In spirit life we can all read the "scripts" and gain an intellectual understanding, but reading the plot is not the same as experiencing the part.

The lovely inspirational Shirley MacLaine effectively summed this up with the title of one of her books, "It's all in the Playing".

"Experiential participation" is the only way to truly absorb the "lessons" that Earth life can teach us.

There are many other sheep that want and even expect beings from another planet to arrive and help to solve all the problems of this world. At the same time, they anticipate that this will give them a better and easier life.

There are other people who have "awakened" to some degree, yet are constantly expecting "new energies" to reach our planet. They seem to think that these will "overnight" awaken everyone so that we all become more enlightened beings.

While I truly do believe and understand that energies that are and will still further raise the consciousness of this planet and every single life form upon her (the planet to some is known as "Gaia"), these 'new higher energies' do take time to integrate and show their effects. I have heard a number of spirit guides speak in confirmation of the higher consciousness energies currently flowing to planet Earth *(See the "Websites and Links" section to find some of these recordings)*. Some Astrologers have also mentioned this. A new golden age is on the cusp of unfolding; how soon may be down to us, and how quickly we can respond to these higher frequency energies. The medium of one spirit guide said it may take 20-30 years to more fully materialise in a clearly positive way.

So those expecting an instant overnight transformation may feel a little disappointed. It would, of course, be lovely to get up one morning and find that everyone on the planet had awoken with higher spiritual awareness. Although, that said, some people may be more open to a speedy personal awakening than others.

But, alas, in most cases an instant awakening would undermine our experiential purpose for incarnation. Intellectually we would become all too conscious of how we *ought* to behave towards each other, rather than developing the emotional desire and mental capacity as a natural aspect of our lower consciousness expansion and growth.

Soul evolution does necessitate that we climb from the bottom rung of the ladder by developing lower mind, before we can climb to the "dizzy" heights of more advanced higher levels of consciousness. At least this is part of the reason why we are here upon Earth at this present time.

One lesson we all need to learn is to follow our own intuitive guidance, rather than waiting for someone or something else to intervene and wave a magic wand (because this will never happen).

We *truly are* the power, we are each our own guru, we *are* all immortal souls; we don't need a "movement" or some special "intervention" to show us the way forward.

The "new age" arrives every morning – every day, every moment is a new beginning.

There is no need or reason, other than as a social gathering, for "new-agers" to get together around some ancient monument at set times and days. Nor any reason to follow any old teachings or rituals.

Every day is special if we make it so. It is our own choice.

24. The Government

My friends, I hardly know where to start when writing about the political system that 'governs' the UK and those "involved".

I also expect that much of what I have to say in this section can be applied to the majority of world governments.

No doubt there are some honourable people involved who live in the hope of making a difference, and of serving society in some way. However, it seems hard to spot the genuine individual.

How can any respect be offered to a system that allows corruption to flourish with only occasional slaps on the wrist?

Yet corruption seems inescapable in a system that embraces "party-line policies".

Every vote taken by Members of Parliament (MP's) is tainted by policy devised or defined by the Prime Minister (PM) and the "Cabinet" – who are basically a limited number of "department heads" selected by the PM.

If any MP rocks the boat by speaking against a particular policy that is proposed by their party it is highly likely that it will go against them in the future. They will certainly forfeit any chance of ever making it into the "inner sanctum" of the cabinet. In other words an unofficial policy of fear and control dominates politics.

It is little wonder that decisions are made which appear to be at odds with the majority. It is because the minority rule.

The general public are, or certainly used to be, indoctrinated with the belief that politicians somehow know best and have our collective interests at heart. Despite a number of politicians' exposure for fraud, such as making false expenses claims, or corruption of one sort or another. *(The blatant corruption of politicians and many others has become all too obvious to vast numbers of people worldwide since 2020).*

The sheep are effectively brainwashed into believing that it's all too complicated for the average person, who merely uses commonsense rather than political "big brother" thinking.

I may (or may not) surprise readers by confessing that I do not have all the answers! But I do believe that a complete political reform is required. I would propose a system with NO political parties.

Instead, I would suggest an election of independent MP's; with those people respected in their area far more likely to be elected. Those people who are genuinely concerned for the good of their own community and society in general. They would have no party-line to follow, only commonsense and their conscience, and the wishes of their community.

The new independent MP's could then select their own committees to oversee national policies. Naturally, they could vote for equally "good spirited individuals" whom they feel to be ideally suited to particular roles, without the fear of future forfeit.

We need a "breed" of politicians capable of leaving aside their egos – the right people with the right motives – not sheep who are "in it" for personal power and fame – or willing to bow to the dictates of one leader or group or the elites of the corporate globalists.

The bottom line in this section is to encourage readers to recognise that they are equal members of the human race whilst on Earth. We are all entitled to an opinion, and should have the right to expect a truly decent person to be elected to represent the community in which we live.

We need to see beyond the facade that allows others to dominate national and world policies. Are such people serving us, have they the good of all at heart? Or are they behaving outside of moral if not literal legal limits for their own personal agenda, profit and power? I think the latter is all too often the case.

In fact, at present as I type this it seems those who are directing life in the UK and in many countries globally are behaving like social-psychopaths who are 'hell bent' on destroying the livelihood and natural health of their citizens. It seems they have 'overnight' signed-up to an agenda to 'jab' every person they possibly can, and as frequently as they can, for no genuine and truthful good reason. They probably believe they will face no consequences, despite the fact that what they are doing has, in my opinion, nothing to do with health and could even lead to a mass reduction in the world population. They, it seems, have no concept or belief or understanding in an 'afterlife' and natural laws and the karma they are for themselves sowing. This, I feel, will certainly propel some of these people to a very, very dark realm of spirit life.

Turning my attention back to the UK, it is also high time that the House of Lords was dissolved.

No free society should be overseen by historic piers, people who have inherited or had a title bestowed upon them. Those who help direct national policies should only be those we have freely elected.

But what can we, individuals, do to help make the change that is necessary?

For a start, as each individual "wakes-up" to better express their higher principles in life and lives by these, they, together with millions doing likewise in this world, instigate a shift in the "collective unconscious" (as it is often called).

When the collective unconscious is raised, all life starts to respond. Not overnight (unfortunately). But gradually, it becomes an inevitable shift in perception and those who live solely for themselves will be exposed for what they are. In a sense, it becomes a "spiritual revolution".

This is happening already. As we empower ourselves by shedding unhelpful indoctrinated habits, this allows us to better express the spirit within. When millions of us do this, collectively, we will help to create a more harmonised world.

Dreams can sometimes come true; no matter what they may be.

They may be personal or for the collective good of us all; or perhaps (and hopefully) for the good of the environment and animals too.

25. 'Royalty'

My friends, personally, I absolutely loathe hearing the so called "English national anthem". Yet whenever England are about to play football I hear the sheep bleating along with it, in the dreadful ritual of singing this so-called English anthem before kick-off.

Quite often the sheep also start up a chorus or two during play; more especially if the team are playing well or winning. It is an anthem that is purely Royalist worship, and does not say a word about supporting the nation.

Historically, those families who have been elevated to the highest position in history so often only got there by defeating and usually killing many others, before they claimed the throne for themselves. (Or they got others to do the 'dirty' work for them!!). They were very often no better than any other world dictator. If anyone got in their way or posed a potential future threat, including members of their own families, they were exiled (if fortunate), otherwise killed.

"Good" kings or queens were only considered good if they didn't tax the common people too highly and generally left them to live their lives in peace.

If the king or queen wanted to wage war on some other nation worth looting, the poor sheep had to contribute financially or through combat – sometimes both.

It bothers me not a jot whether any current 'royal' is a nice person or not, the whole system that embraces a monarchy is archaic, and should be left in the realms of children's fantasy stories. It also fosters the class system which embraces greed. This is far removed from loving spiritual virtues, fairness and goodness.

How can a society that is capable of space travel and unravelling truths about the universe and other dimensions of life, knowing that all are morally born equal, still be capable of calling someone sovereign, prince or princess and so forth, and prostrating themselves before such a person?

Do sheep people admire them because such people had ancestors who were capable of greater collusion, manipulation and ruthless cruelty?

Because these were the kind of "attributes" they historically required to enable them to defeat others and claim authority.

Perhaps it is because the sheepish fail to recognise how absurd the whole system is?

Therefore they continue in the same way that their ancestors did; afraid to question, or too apathetic to even consider their own thoughts and actions.

I used to think that Charles seemed a reasonable person, but I must say that my feelings about him have deteriorated significantly in recent times. It seems to me that he, like so many others, is linked to what can be called the dark global agenda. Although, ultimately, this agenda will never obliterate the light of spirit and truth reaching evermore people upon this planet.

I would still have no trouble having a chat with Charles, or with anyone whom, I may to some degree, be able to enlighten. However, I'd prefer to do this "down the pub" while having a casual pint of beer, just the two of us, rather than in Buckingham Palace or the like surrounded by secret service security guards on standby to pounce or attack if I reached into my pocket unexpectedly.

The life of a 'royal' gives them financial security, but at what cost to their personal freedom? I think it is high time the sheep came to their senses and relieved them of such responsibility.

We would really be doing them and their future generations a huge favour. They could gracefully retire and start spending their personal fortunes helping others (at least that would be my suggestion to them).

We all need to wake up and recognise the stupidity of putting others on a pedestal and effectively worshipping them – whoever they are. We are each as good as anyone but no greater. Likewise, those deemed "royalty" are no better or more special than anyone else. There should be no titles, Lords, Knights of the realm and so forth. It is a system to maintain a 'class system' that promotes inequality.

I can add, I have heard former Queens, Victoria and Alexandra communicating from spirit life to say that their former titles, now that they are in the spirit world, mean nothing to them. In spirit we are all equal, and it is the status of our soul that determines our place in spirit life. *(See 'Website and Links' section to find these and more direct voice spirit recordings).*

I realise that the so-called 'royal' may only be 'playing a role' in their earthly life, but is it also a soul opportunity for them to challenge the unfair nature of the system into which they have incarnated? Perhaps their higher self might wish so, but can this or a spirit guide sufficiently 'get through' to their earthly conscience?

Diana, in her own kind way, did most certainly challenge the system. I have no proof, but I do not for one second believe that her physical death was an accident. Yet, of course, the higher self is often 'happy' to welcome home to spirit life the earthly aspect. Furthermore, NDE accounts reaffirm to us that going home is a great joy, and not a sorrow. Although, of course, it may bring sadness to loved ones left on Earth and, especially so, if they have no concept or belief in the 'afterlife'.

26. Bigger Issues

The essence of part two of this book naturally encourages everyone to *be themselves on Earth*. As we do so, perhaps it is a natural progression to also think with greater intuitive awareness of some of the *bigger issues* of this world?

When we do start to really question what is going on in this world, to degree we may also, and quite naturally, help to make a difference.

To begin with, as we shine our inner light of reason on some of the bigger issues, we soon realise the stupidity of us collectively continuing in a certain way. When we recognise this, we can also add our voice to the call for change.

There are a great number of "bigger issues" that could be put under our spotlight. I have no intention of going into great detail on each. But I will briefly touch on a few.

Crime rates do fluctuate; some go down in numbers while other crimes are on the increase. But in general it seems to me that as the years roll past more and more crimes are committed.

One could ask why? Is it the inequality of society? Partially, and absolutely this is a major factor.

However, prisons in the UK and all over the world are full of people who were never taught the truth about life. That is, they like most people were never taught that life is a spirit experience that takes place in a physical body. Also, and more importantly, that our actions bring consequences that can outweigh and have a longer impact than a prison sentence.

I wonder just how many people, who have been or at present are, in prisons, if from childhood we were all

taught the spirit facts of life, would have lived completely different and more fulfilling lives?

Do we also do enough to re-educate prison inmates? I, unfortunately, doubt it; because so much of society is 'the blind leading the blind', as the old proverb says.

The next issue I wish to mention is military weapons, and particularly those that can greatly devastate the world. Many people say that these effectively are for our own protection; as a threat to deter others from attacking us.

Yet I can't help but feel that simply by having such weapons we acknowledge our own fears and insecurities, and show our lack of spirit awareness. What are we afraid of, we are immortal spirit beings.

However, we perhaps need all nations to acknowledge our spirit nature, and not simply the odd one or two in isolation. Then we might all disarm?

To begin with, it would naturally help greatly if we in the UK as a nation, along with the USA, stopped invading other nations. Then perhaps they, and their people, would have fewer quarrels with us in the first place?

The present state of this world and the actions instigated by certain people is so sad to see. When, as investigators tell us, we follow the "money trail" of mega-wealthy corporations we see that they have manipulated and helped to fund so much that is cruel and unwarranted in this world.

The evidence informs us that they have literally instigated and funded wars in order to gain control over the affairs of other nations for their own power and profit. I have heard that there have even been cases where certain corporate giants have sold weapons to both sides!

Those in 'control' and pulling the strings of these acts of inhumanity are always physically secure in safe environments. Yet, of course, they live in spirit and spiritual ignorance, and fail to see the long term consequences that they are karmically creating for themselves. As I have said, it is sad. No one can prevent karma from fulfilling itself, whether in spirit life this initially brings us joy or misery.

The catalogue of sad, inhumane, and karmically negative offences to fairness and decency include destroying ancient forests for cheap grazing or the growth of unnecessary crops. In doing so, they have shown zero concern, or care or consideration, for the plant and animal life of the forests.

Furthermore, I believe that they (the people responsible) have held back cheaper and eco-friendly systems in favour of fossil fuel production because they make ever-greater fortunes from these. Again, they do so with no regard for the consequences to the planet, the environment, and the eco-system, and plant, animal or human life.

The same or similar people from behind the scenes are responsible for spraying crops and killing vital insects and wildlife such as bees. Others (or perhaps the same people) are also spraying the skies in "climate control experiments", or "geo-engineering" as it is sometimes called, with no way of knowing the long-term consequences.

- *The current dark agenda blames fossil fuels and the populace of the world for so-called "climate change". While I have zero love for cars having never owned one, and will be glad to see an end to all unnecessary use of fossil fuels, they have nothing to do with the global temperature. The 'agenda' it seems to me is using this 'excuse' as justification for their actions and to manipulate certain gullible people to 'go along' with their plans. The reason it seems why the global temperature rises periodically, is linked to solar flares. In other words it is the Sun that determines our temperature and climate. The temperature rises then fall in cycles that can last for hundreds of years.*

Other giant corporations or conglomerates run the pharmaceutical industry that seems hell bent on more or less what I consider 'poisoning' every person on the planet with unnecessary and harmful drugs and jabs. At least this is how it seems to me.

Once again if the evidence is pursued it shows that the early drug industry lobbied and in one way or another harassed, purchased or caused the closure of their forerunners, the herbalists. Even what is now "Boots the Chemist" (in the UK) was originally, "Boots the Herbalists" having begun trading in Nottingham in 1849 with the opening of a single herbalist shop.

The power and manipulative control of the pharmaceutical industry enables 'them' (who don't realise the karma) to block the development or sale of safe alternatives to their drugs. This includes alternative, drug free, treatments for cancer. They make far more money when people remain ill, especially with never-ending repeat prescriptions. Whereas, genuine cures would more or less put them out of business, or greatly decrease their sales and therefore profits. This is especially so with natural treatments that come from nature and can sometimes be grown in people's gardens or greenhouses.

The list of "crimes against humanity" these shameless corporations instigate seems endless. Yet no matter how much they destroy, life *is* immortal and natural spirit laws cannot be bypassed.

- **Those responsible are really damaging themselves most of all. It seems obvious to me that they have no understanding of the natural laws of this Universe. If they did, they would realise how they will one day have to redress the negative karma that they are, without a doubt, creating for themselves.**

But of course this isn't the way life on Earth should, or at least could, be.

When a sufficient number of people "wake-up" and start to respond to all these atrocities, we will see change, it will be inevitable. This is so because it is the majority who really hold the power. When they use it, everything changes.

I would encourage all freethinkers to enlighten others in regard to these outrages (and any others they know about) and to send out their thoughts (prayers) for things to change.

When prayers, thoughts and ideas and wishes for change are sent out into the collective unconscious this does lay the foundation to bring about change. Eventually it triggers a shift in conscious awareness. The "collective unconscious" is the name given to the mental field of energy that incorporates this planet. We all link to this because, at the 'end of day', we are all energetically connected spirit beings. We are all facets or aspects of the same energy we generally call, "God".

Thoughts that reach the collective unconscious can awaken within our conscious minds; this could be compared to how a subject under hypnosis awakens memories of their childhood, or even a past life.

This is happening already, and all around the world; people *are* "waking up". It isn't necessary to take my word for anything, information is 'out there' online (although fake news exists too), and there are many people discussing these things.

Naturally, there are still those sheepish people with their heads in the sand believing all the exposures that are taking place are "conspiracy theories". But I'm certain that everything I have mentioned is based on truth. In fact, what I have said is only the tip of the iceberg.

My main purpose for including this section herein is to say that as well as expressing ourselves and living our lives in a way that is truthful and honest and respectful of ourselves, and to not blindly follow the flock mentality, is to add that if we see unfairness, cruelty and so forth in this world then we need also to respond to this in a way that is faithful to the soul we are.

We are, after all, part of the whole.

Shortly there is a quote from the spirit guide *White Feather* that is relevant to this section. *Robert Goodwin* is a friend and the medium through whom the guide speaks, and some of Robert's books are mentioned in my recommended reading list. He also has a website:

https://www.whitefeatherspirit.com/

Here is the quote:

> *"Were humanity to fully awaken to realise its individual and collective power, your world would be transformed. As things stand, the few dictate to the many who, in their semi-sleep state, follow like sheep and seldom think to question for themselves. Quite clearly this needs to be addressed, and each thinking reasoning person, should play their part in helping to quicken the collective awareness of the race.*

It is abhorrent to witness the beauty of creation being destroyed by greed and ignorance and it is time for the warriors of truth to make their voices heard.

I sometimes think that I am a lone voice in the wilderness whose words are drowned out by the cacophony of corporate rhetoric that spews forth from the human ego. Yet I know for certain that I must continue operating as I do to enlighten the gentle, discerning souls whose ears arrest my discourse.

If we can awaken one, amongst the millions, then our efforts are vindicated. If however, we are able, with the help of those who are brave enough to go against the flow and stand up for the truth, to touch many whose minds are ripe for knowledge, then a great victory for light over darkness and truth over ignorance is achievable.

Play your part. Do not shirk the responsibility that your spiritual understanding has given you. Do not wait for your brother to speak out on your behalf. Speak your truth now. Shout it from the rooftop if you have to but do so in the certain knowledge that you are a force for goodness and light in a world that grows darker by the minute."

I wish to ensure that this section, although containing some rather negative information, also includes sufficient positive narrative to ensure that the negative info does not depress anyone. So once more I remind every reader that, **life is eternal**. We are all immortal spirit beings. We can only do our best whilst we are on Earth. So let's do just that, and make a difference; for our own sake, and for the sake of others.

The following are some changes I think would help to create a better world; and perhaps when more people are spiritually awake, some of these will be considered. Some of these apply exclusively to the UK, but most can be taken on board worldwide. They are not in any particular order of importance.

1. The closure of all "Stock Exchanges or Markets"

They generate greed and lead to vested interests. They may be 'useful' for determining the value of certain commodities, or crops, but surely this can be achieved without 'investors' profiteering in share values (or however this works). It all smacks of greed and not of fairness to, in the case of crops, farmers.

As for 'limited' companies, I suggest no more than ten people to hold a share in any company. I have grave reservations in regard to the 'limited' aspect to, this, I feel needs to be seriously looked at by sensible people with no greed or vested interests in maintaining a system that can, so it seems, be too easily 'played' for personal benefit. There have been all too many cases of people 'draining' a company of its financial value then 'going broke' (bankrupt) while one or more directors or their families have, directly or indirectly through the resources of the company, 'fortunes' in their banks or assets (property, etc.).

2. The Cessation of "Patents"

If someone doesn't want to share something freely they are inventing (or whatever) for the wrong reasons. People should be proud to make a discovery or invent something for the good of all and not expect to 'forever' be rewarded. If only they would realise that all inspiration they receive comes from the spirit realms; whether it be from a spirit scientist, doctor, writer, musician, or their own higher-self or anyone else it is given to them freely to share.

I see nothing wrong with someone being presented with some sort of award and / or even one-off cash reward, to go along with public appreciation. But I do not feel it is right for anyone to 'forever' receive some percentage or royalty with the right to prosecute someone who repeats or adds or comes along with something derived from the original idea.

3. The teaching of genuine spirit facts

I would like to see genuine spirit communications and explanations to 'how this Universe works', 'the meaning of life', and so much more, made available to the public from childhood.

It is time to leave behind the vested interest and misunderstanding caused by so many world religions. With teachings that have for centuries simply caused confusion in the minds of so, so many, while tying them to some archaic, outdated belief or ritual.

4. The abolition of the monarchy in the UK

(As mentioned earlier in this book)

It is ridiculous that anyone or any family should be elevated to such fame and fortune for no good reason, and (it seems) be subject to different rules that place them separate and above the average person.

5. No more salaries that are excessive while others can barely feed themselves or family

(Again, as touched upon within)

It should be remembered that we are each valuable unique individualised spirit beings.

6. No more over-ruling the public and majority

I believe that referendums should be used to make every major decision. It should not be down to the elected 'few' who have so often proven themselves untrustworthy and self-seeking.

7. No more "Official Secrets"

We elect people who are answerable to us and expect them to behave responsibly. They have no right or authority to hide things from us and should do nothing without our consent.

8. There should be no Internet use of a User Name or Alias to hide an identity

This one may seem a bit like 'big brother'? However, in a fair and open society I feel we should all be able to comment (such as on social media) without the need to hide one's identity. Having seen documentaries about how paedophiles manage to sign-up to child chat rooms so easily with a user name and to then groom their future victims it seems outrageous in this day and age that an alias can so easily be used. It is likewise the situation with many cases of online verbal (typed) abuse. If someone wants to make a comment they should be obliged to do so in their own name and for everyone to know that it truly is the individual they claim to be.

Of course, if someone does not want anyone to know what they think or feel about anything then they need not comment!

No doubt there are plenty more that could be added to the above eight, but this list is a start.

There are many more 'big issues' under scrutiny in this world at this time. I will perhaps address some of these in a further book. But for now, I would like to remind reads what we should all know, and never forget for even a second, that is, **that life is eternal.**

I believe we should all make every effort to really get to know ourselves by thinking deeply about life and how and why we react as we do.

Sages say, "Go within" through meditation; this (meditation) could also be termed deep contemplation. It is through such practises that clarity and revelations, a sudden "knowing" comes to mind, and this could be about anything.

Whether we receive any personal revelations or not we should at all times endeavour to 'honour ourselves' (be ourselves), and be true to ourselves, to our spirit nature, by living and expressing ourselves in ways that are in harmony with our real spirit nature. This means we should be expressing love, kindness, compassion, forgiveness, and all other virtues. We are sovereign beings, free spirits, immortal co-creators within the universe, as such, we should be living without fear, without yielding to impositions and dictates that are out of alignment with natural and spirit law.

So I say once more…

Know Thyself.

Be Thyself.

Final Thoughts

My friends, speaking generally, I would suggest that to *truly* "*be thyself*" and an authentic and sensible example of this whilst on Earth we need to engage our "psychic sense"; in other words, our "intuition". My advice is to always follow its direction, together with what the heart tells us, and this is our inner conscience speaking to us.

I sincerely hope that what I have had to say has or will encourage every reader to be (or remain) a freethinker – and to always **be true to their inner self**.

We can all seem like sheep at times, but there is a big difference between doing as others do when our higher mind encourages this, and doing so as an unenlightened sheep, who does not really think freely, and remains tied to the flock mentality.

This is why I encourage everyone who is willing to listen, to feel, with their heart, soul and intuition, which pathway this directs them to follow. It may be a similar pathway to the one taken by many others, but it may also be unique in its own right, and if it is, this is fine.

We can only ever do our best during Earth life. If we harm no one deliberately, and can find it within ourselves to willingly and happily help others when we feel able to do so, with due respect to our own needs, nobody could ever ask more of themselves.

We should endeavour to at all times remember that we are all unique immortal individualised souls; and that each of us is capable of thinking and acting as one at all times. So let's all do so.

Naturally, our eternal destiny is, and always will be, in our own hands.

Addresses

The Spiritualists' National Union
Redwoods, Stansted Hall,
Stansted, Essex, CM24 8UD
Tele: 01279 816363
www.snu.org.uk

The Spiritualist Association of Great Britain
341 Queenstown Road, Battersea,
London, SW8 4LH
Tele: 0207 931 6488
www.sagb.org.uk

The Greater World Christian Spiritualist Organisation
3-5 Conway Street, Fitzrovia,
London W1T 6BJ
Tele: 020 7436 7555
www.greaterworld.net

Psychic News (Monthly magazine)
Unit 2, Griggs Business Centre,
West Street, Coggeshall,
Essex, CO6 1NT
Tele: 01376 563091
www.psychicnews.org.uk

Websites and Links

Spiritist & Spiritualist

www.snu.org.uk – The Spiritualists' National Union
www.sagb.org.uk – Spiritualist Association of Great Britain
http://bussuk.webs.com – British Union of Spiritist Societies
www.ism.org.uk – The Institute of Spiritualist Mediums
www.greaterworld.net – Christian Spiritualists
www.whiteagle.org – White Eagle
www.silverbirchpublishing.co.uk – Silver Birch (books)

Spiritual Healing

www.harryedwardshealingsanctuary.org.uk
www.thehealingtrust.org.uk – Nat. Fed. Of Spiritual Healers
https://ministrymoe.org - Stephen Turoff, Healer-Surgeon
http://raybrownhealing.com – Healer-Surgeon
www.spiritsurgeon.co.uk – Ed Pearson

Trance Mediums

www.whitefeatherspirit.com – Robert Goodwin
www.suzannegiesemann.com - Suzanne Giesemann
www.kevinryerson.com – Kevin Ryerson

Physical Mediums

www.scottmilligan.net

Spiritual Mediums-Artists

www.sandyingham.co.uk

NDE Links

https://iands.org – Int. Association for Near-death Studies
www.anitamoorjani.com – Anita Moorjani
http://ebenalexander.com – Eben Alexander

Magazines
http://psychicnews.org.uk

Animal Communicators
www.ameliakinkade.com
www.animalspirit.org - Anna Breytenbach

Spirit Voice Recordings
A collection of spirit voice recordings:
www.leslieflint.com
Queen Victoria speaking:
https://www.leslieflint.com/victoria-and-john-brown
Queen Alexandra - Speaking from the Spirit World:
https://www.youtube.com/watch?v=Nk88LAH7lgc&t=3s
Leslie Flint Tribute Webpage
https://leslieflinttribute.mystrikingly.com/

Other Informative Links
www.iisis.net – Reincarnation Research
www.spr.ac.uk – Society for Psychical Research
www.windbridge.org – Studying dying, death and what next
www.sheldrake.org – Science and Spiritual
www.lucistrust.org – Alice Bailey books etc.
www.victorzammit.com – Scientific Evidence and Much More

Find Truth
This webpage contains links to a number of spirit guides
speaking: https://findtruth.mystrikingly.com/

Recommended Reading

My Top Recommendation

Victor & Wendy Zammit - *A Lawyer Presents the Evidence for the Afterlife*

Some of My Personal Favourites

Allan Kardec - *The Spirit's Book*

Brian Sadler - *The Meaning and Purpose of Life*

Irene Sowter - *Tails to Tell - The Extraordinary Experiences of an Animal Healer*

Kevin Ryerson and Stephanie Harolde - *Spirit Communication-The Soul's Path*

Robert & Amanda Goodwin - Three titles (from many) - *In the Presence of White Feather - The Enlightened Soul – The Collected Wisdom of White Feather*

Other Highly Recommended

Alice Bailey - *The Consciousness of the Atom*

Anita Moorjani – Dying to be Me - My journey from cancer, to near-death, to true healing (NDE experience)

Anthony Borgia - Three books (from many) - *Life in the World Unseen - More about Life in the World Unseen - Here and Hereafter*

Arthur Findlay – Two titles (from many) - *The Rock of Truth – The Curse of Ignorance*

Barry Eaton – Past Lives Unveiled

Carol Bowman - *Return from Heaven* (Reincarnation within the same family)

Eben Alexander - *Proof of Heaven* (NDE experience)

Emma Hardinge Britten – *The Faiths, Facts and Frauds of Religious History*

Felicity Joan Medland - *Life around My Father Harry Edwards*

Frederick C. Sculthorp - *Excursions to the Spirit World* (Astral Projection)

Gary E. Schwartz Ph.D. - *The Afterlife Experiments - Breakthrough Scientific Evidence of Life after Death*

Ivy Northage - Two titles: *Journey Beyond* (Trance talks by Chan); *Spiritual Realisation* (Communicated by Chan)

Leslie Flint – *Voices in the Dark - My Life as a Medium*

Lynne McTaggart - *The Field* (Scientific investigations)

Michael Newton - Two titles - *Journey of Souls - Destiny of Souls*

Neville Randall – *Life After Death*

N. Riley Heagerty – The Hereafter

Paul Miller - *Faces of the Living Dead* (The amazing psychic art of Frank Leah)

Penny Sartori (Dr) – *The Wisdom of Near-Death Experiences*

Ramus Branch - *Harry Edwards - The life story of the great healer*

Raymond Smith - Sir Oliver Lodge spirit group (one of three) - *The Truth the Whole Truth and Nothing but the Truth*

Robin P. Foy - *In Pursuit of Physical Mediumship*

Silver Birch - Three titles (from many) - *Silver Birch Anthology - The Seed of Truth - Light from Silver Birch*

Stephen Turoff - *Seven Steps to Eternity*

Ursula Roberts - Two titles: *Wisdom of Ramadahn - More Wisdom of Ramadahn*

White Eagle – Two titles (from many) - *Walking with the Angels - Spiritual Unfoldment 2*

About the Author

James McQuitty was born in Putney, London in 1950, and worked there for many years before moving to Ryde, Isle of Wight, UK in 1992.

He began to seriously study spiritual philosophy in 1981, and at this time he also began to regularly attend demonstrations by the renowned medium *Jessie Nason*.

Since then he has had many personal experiences and seen spirit visitors on numerous occasions, as well as receiving a great number of spirit communications via other mediums. These include a trance communication message that led to him becoming an author, with the release of his first book in 1994.

In his books he shares an understanding of our true status in this universe, which is that of immortal souls, and much, much more.

His writing style is easy to read and understand, enabling even those who are new to the subjects covered to finish highly informed and greatly inspired.

Printed in Great Britain
by Amazon